5·50

PROFESSOR R. W. FOGEL
HARVARD UNIVERSITY
1737 CAMBRIDGE ST., RM.
CAMBRIDGE, MA. 02138

5/12/78

POPULATION AND DISEASE
IN EARLY INDUSTRIAL ENGLAND

PIONEERS OF DEMOGRAPHY

A series of collective reprints of the more important milestones in the development of historical demography.

THIS SERIES INCLUDES:

The earliest classics: John Graunt and Gregory King
Mortality in pre-industrial times: the contemporary verdict
Enclosure and population
The population of Ireland before the 19th century
Population and disease in early industrial England
Comparative statistics in the 19th century
Slum conditions in London and Dublin
Mortality in mid 19th century Britain
Rates of mortality
J.-B. Bertrand: *A historical relation of the plague at Marseilles in the year 1720*
T. Short: *Comparative history of the increase and decrease of mankind*
T. Short: *New observations on city, town and country bills of mortality*
W. Black: *An arithmetical and medical analysis of the diseases and mortality of the human species*
E. H. Greenhow: *Papers relating to the sanitary state of the people of England* (General Board of Health Papers)

Each volume contains a new introduction.

POPULATION AND DiSEASE
IN EARLY INDUSTRIAL ENGLAND

T. Percival

OBSERVATIONS ON THE STATE OF POPULATION IN MANCHESTER

(1789)

W. Heberden

OBSERVATIONS ON THE INCREASE AND DECREASE

OF DIFFERENT DISEASES

AND PARTICULARLY OF THE PLAGUE

(1801)

T. Percival

ESSAY ON THE SMALL-POX AND MEASLES

(1789)

With an introduction

by

B. BENJAMIN

1973

GREGG INTERNATIONAL PUBLISHERS LIMITED

ISBN 0 576 53288 6

Printed in Germany

INTRODUCTION

William Heberden, the younger, born in 1767 was the second and only sur-
viving son of William Heberden (1710–1801) an eminent physician and
scientist, whom Dr. Johnson described as the 'last of our learned physicians'
but whose work was such that he might have been described as the first of the
moderns. The younger Heberden was also a distinguished scholar and an
accomplished physician. Like his father he became a Fellow of the Royal
Society. Early in life he was attached to the court and became physician in
ordinary to the Queen in 1806 and to the King in 1809. He had a large practice. In 1812, however, his wife died, leaving him with nine children to whose
education he thereafter almost wholly devoted himself apart from attendance
on the King. In 1829 one of his sons died while still a medical student and a
daughter died shortly afterwards. Heberden then retired altogether from
medical practice and devoted himself to theology until his death in 1845.

His observations on diseases are prefaced by an 'advertisement' reminiscent
of Graunt. 'The author is influenced by no vanity. . . . His object is to direct
the attention of the medical world to a subject which has hitherto been much
neglected – the Bills of Mortality. The Bills, admits Heberden, have certain
defects (they include only those baptised in the Church of England; some of
those so baptised are buried without Bills; abortions and still births are
excluded; there is vagueness in certification of disease) but careful observations may still, he urges, extract valuable knowledge. In fact, Heberden's
suggestion that the Bills had been neglected was not justified, but he thought
them to be and, in the event, it was as well that he did so, since it spurred
him to a valuable series of observations.

Two tables are presented. One shows for each year from 1701 to 1800, for
London, the number of christenings and burials and the proportion (out of
every thousand deaths) who died from bowel complaints, smallpox, palsy,
measles or childbirth. The other table shows, also for London, the variations
week by week in the years 1763–67, 1795–99, of deaths (all ages), deaths
under two, deaths over 60, sudden deaths, deaths from childbirth, consump-
tion, fever, bowel conditions, measles and smallpox.

Heberden then proceeds to comment on these tables, remarking on the rise
in mortality up to 1720 and the gradual decline after 1750. Christenings were
at their lowest between 1740 and 1760 and thereafter gradually increased.
More people, he noticed even then, were moving out of London to more
open conditions. He was very much struck by the decline in 'dysentery'
deaths (griping in the guts, colic, blood flux) from an annual average of 1,070
in 1700–10 to an average of 20 in 1790–1800, and attributes this decline to
improved cleanliness and ventilation. (It has to be borne in mind, however,
that the great authority on epidemics, Charles Creighton, was of the opinion

that this decline was not nearly as remarkable as the Bills seem to suggest.) Smallpox vaccination, Heberden alleged, protected the rich but preserved a constant reservoir of infection for the unprotected poor. 'This must always be an objection against making any great city the place for inoculation until the practice is become universal among all ranks of the people'. This was an unjustifiable assertion and was based on a misconception as to the infectiousness of vaccinated persons and of the disease-producing power of the vaccine, neither of which was high. But, at that time, for whatever reason, he was right to press for universality. However, while deaths of smallpox were, in total, increasing, the following comparison was duly noted by Heberden:

	Smallpox death rate per 100
Inoculated	2·5
Uninoculated	160

Sudden deaths as a proportion of all deaths doubled during the 18th century. Heberden was not happy with conjectures about alcohol or tea or other dietary changes but he confessed to being unable to offer any alternative suggestion.

Part II of the volume refers to the plague and begins with a table showing weekly deaths in the worst plague years of 1593, 1603, 1625, 1636, and 1665. As Heberden remarks, 'a melancholy picture'. The 'headquarters' of plague had always been 'the nastiest part of dirty, crowded, ill-constructed large cities.' He cites Cairo as an example and refers to the pollution of the Nile. But, he argues, whatever its origin, the disease had been propagated in London with its open drains and poor ventilation. He refers to the 'most gracious blessing' of the fire of London in 1666 which allowed rebuilding and a remedy of the worst conditions: ' . . . in a few years the new town rose up like a phoenix from the fire with increased vigour and beauty. Nor did the benefit end there; for it produced in the country a spirit of improvement which had till then been unknown, but which has never since ceased to exert itself'. In 1665, there were 68,000 plague deaths; in 1666, 2,000; in 1667, 35; in 1668, 14; and, in 1669, 5. The last year that was mentioned at all was 1679. Heberden considers whether the disease may have worn itself out but on the basis of overseas evidence, discounts this suggestion. 'Our long exemption from the plague is not so much to be attributed to any . . . absence of its exciting cause as to our own change of manners . . . '.

In a general sense Heberden was right; the plague was eradicated by environmental improvement and especially by cleanliness. However, his interpretation of the origin of outbreaks of plague was false and too much orientated to the old 'miasma' theory of infection – that, somehow, breathing the atmosphere of dirty smelly places could convey disease. It has to be remembered that Heberden was writing long before the development of bacteriology and even before there was general suspicion that diseases like the plague were water- or food-borne.

Percival's two essays were published in 1789. Their author, Thomas Percival, was born in Warrington in Lancashire in 1740 and died in Manchester in 1804. Both his parents died when he was three years old and he was left to the care of an elder sister. When he was ten, his uncle (also a Thomas Percival) who was a physician, died and left him a small income and a valuable library. The young boy decided to qualify in medicine and went first to school in Warrington and then to Edinburgh University. While still a student he visited London and made the acquaintance of many scientific people. In consequence he was elected a Fellow of the Royal Society (it was alleged that no one had previously been elected at so young an age). From Edinburgh he went to Leyden where he completed his medical studies in 1765. After two years of practice in Warrington (during which time he married) he moved to Manchester where he remained for the rest of his life, abandoning an original intention to go to London.

Percival and Heberden had differences and similarities. Both were medical men, both were inclined to scientific enquiry. However, while Heberden enjoyed a wealthy practice and indulged his scientific curiosity (to good purpose), Percival, though not by any means poor, was more dependent on his practice, had closer contact with ordinary people and perhaps for that reason had more of a social conscience. He was not content with satisfying curiosity; he wanted to translate knowledge to political action. Because of his practical approach he was probably sounder in his conclusions.

Percival made an early reputation by contributing papers to 'philosophical transactions' and other periodicals. His essays, medical and experimental, issued in 1767–76 attracted wide attention. In 1775 he published the first of three parts of 'A Father's Instructions'; the concluding part was not issued until 1800. This book, comprising tales and fables to ensure that children received a moral education, gained great popularity.

He was very concerned with the growing working population of Manchester, with working conditions and with poverty. He helped to form a committee to enforce proper sanitation. He pressed for the establishment of public baths and for improvement (by law) of factory conditions. He was also active intellectually and formed the Manchester Literary and Philosophical Society in 1781.

These present essays show Percival's interest in the effects on health of increasing urbanisation. His approach, like that of Graunt over a hundred years earlier, was to look for regularities and divergencies in statistical series to question their origin. He had a wide circle of friends and acquaintances who, knowing of his interest, sent him statistical summaries based on baptisms and burials of local areas in the Manchester district and sometimes far afield.

Percival looked at age distributions, sex ratios, birth rates, death rates, especially child mortality, the size of families and households. (Child mortality worried him particularly – 'Half the children who are born in Manchester die under five years old.') He related these figures to the urban character of the area, and the predominant occupations: 'So baleful is the influence of large towns on the duration of life; and so justly are they styled . . . the graves of mankind.' He thought that parents were so keen to get their children to work in the factories that they treated them less kindly than horses and cattle: 'The age of gaiety is spent in the midst of tears, punishments and slavery . . . and this to answer no other end but to make a child a man some years before nature intended he should be one.'

Percival did observe that the conditions of the poor were improving with the prosperity of the country; that the poor were getting warmer clothing and better food, especially more wheat (formerly unknown to them) and potatoes; that this was helping to reduce mortality. He also noticed that the birth rate was rising because the increase of trade gave greater encouragement to marriage.

In remarking on the fact that the mortality of males was in every period of life greater than females, especially at birth or soon after, Percival observes that 'male foetuses, being larger, require more nutrition than female foetuses during gestation; and are more liable to injury at the time of birth'.

In those days tuberculosis, regularly, and smallpox, periodically, took very heavy toll of life and in the second of these two essays, Percival turns to compare the lethality of smallpox with the lesser toll of measles, in Manchester. Of all births, 1 in 9 died of smallpox, 1 in 52 of measles. He noticed that while the total of deaths from all causes was fairly stable, the contribution of smallpox fluctuated from year to year. He was shrewd enough to observe that while most of the smallpox deaths were of children under the age of five, there were very few cases in the first three months of life; that there were few cases of *any* infectious disease under three months and that such young infants did not even erupt from smallpox vaccinations. The next eighteen months of age was however a very different story. Three-fifths of all deaths from smallpox occurred in this period. He recommended therefore 2–3 months of age as the best time for vaccination.

I wish says, Percival, 'rather to excite than to anticipate inquiries of the intelligent reader'. A modest claim, more than justified.

Bernard Benjamin
July 1973

E S S A Y I.

OBSERVATIONS ON THE

ȘTATE OF POPULATION

I N

M A N C H E S T E R,

AND OTHER ADJACENT PLACES*(a)*.

FROM an account taken in 1717, the number of inhabitants in Man-chefter, for I am uncertain whether Salford *(b)* was included, appears to have been 8000.

By a furvey made in 1757 of Manchefter and Salford, the number of inhabitants was

(a) Inferted in the Philofophical Tranfactions, vol. LXIV. LXV. LXVI.

(b) MANCHESTER and SALFORD, though diftinguifhed by different names, like London, Weftminfter, and the Borough of Southwark, may be confidered as one and the fame town, being divided only by a fmall river, over which two bridges are erected.

VOL. II.   B   found

found to be 19839. And from 1754 to 1761 inclusive, the number of deaths amounted to 5769. The annual deaths therefore, at the period of the survey, must have been 721, exclusive of dissenters. It is probable, as will appear afterwards, that these would have increased the number to 771. At this time therefore 1 in 25 .7 of the inhabitants of Manchester died every year.

A NEW survey of Manchester has been executed this summer (1773) with great care and accuracy, of which the following is a particular account.

MANCHESTER.		SALFORD.
3402	Houses	866.
5317	Families	1099.
10548	Males	2248.
11933	Females	2517.
7724	Married	1775.
432	Widowers	89.
1064	Widows	149.
7782	Under 15	1793.
3252	Above 50	640.
342	Male Lodgers	18.
150	Female ditto	13.
44	Empty Houses	26.

FROM hence it appears that the number of tenanted houses in Manchester and Salford amounts

amounts to 4268; the families to 6416; and
the inhabitants to 27,246. The proportion of
perfons to a houfe therefore is more than $6\frac{1}{3}$;
and of individuals to a family about $4\frac{1}{4}$. The
females exceed the males by 1654; the wi-
dows are more than double the number of
widowers; and about a feventh part of the
inhabitants have attained the age of fifty.

The following Table is formed from the
Regifter of Burials and Baptifms at the Collegiate or Parifh Church in Manchefter, and
gives the annual number of each on an average.

		Burials.	Baptifms.
From 1580 to 1587 inclufive,		184	
1680	1687	286	
1720	1727	359	
1754	1760	736	769
1761	1765	731	843
1766	1770	870	970

But it fhould be remarked, that this account
does not include the deaths or births amongft the
diffenters. Thefe, by a late improvement in
our Bills of Mortality, are now received into the
Parifh Regifter; and laft year (1772) the former amounted to 50, the latter to 181. Admitting thefe to be the average of unregiftered
baptifms and burials in Manchefter, the annual
medium of deaths from 1768 to 1772 inclufive,

will

will be 958. And the annual births during the
fame period, with the like allowance, will be
1098. Hence the prefent proportion of annual
deaths to the inhabitants is nearly as 1 to 28 .4;
and of births to the inhabitants almoft as 1 to 25.
The births alfo, it appears, exceed the burials
140 every year at a medium.

THE rapid growth of Manchefter is fufficiently
evident from the preceding facts. Yet Leverpool, during the fame fpace of time, has increafed in a much greater proportion. This
appears from the following Table, which I have
extracted from a very curious and entertaining
work, lately publifhed by my ingenious friend
the Rev. Dr. Enfield, Lecturer on the Belles
Lettres in the Academy at Warrington.

(c) Year.	Number of Inhabitants.	Annual Addition.
1700	5714	
1710	8168	245
1720	10446	227
1730	12074	162
1740	18086	601
1750	22099	401
1760	25787	368
1770	34004	822

(c) Hiftory of Leverpool, page 28, fecond edition,
corrected.

ACCORDING

ACCORDING to this Table, Leverpool has at
prefent upwards of fix times the number of inhabitants which it contained at the beginning of
the century.

BUT the progrefs of trade and opulence in
Manchefter has been more than adequate to its
advancement in population. For a confiderable
part of the manufactory of this flourifhing town,
is carried on in the adjacent country, which is
thereby crowded with houfes and inhabitants.
So populous are the environs of Manchefter,
that every houfe in the townfhip has been found,
by a late furvey, to contain, at an average, fix
perfons. The townfhip is indeed but of fmall
extent; and the greateft part of it will probably,
in a fhort time, be included in Manchefter.   It
contains 311 houfes; 361 famil'es; 947 males;
958 females; 656 married perfons; 21 widowers;
42 widows; 763 under 15 years of age; and 222
above 50.

IT is pleafing to obferve, that, notwithftanding
the enlargement of Manchefter, there has been a
fenfible improvement in the healthinefs and
longevity of its inhabitants; for the proportion
of deaths is now confiderably lefs than in 1757.
But this is chiefly to be afcribed, as Dr. Price
has juftly obferved *(d)*, to the large acceffion of

(d) SEE a moft valuable Treatife on Reverfionary Payments, p. 188, third edition.

new

new fettlers from the country. For as thefe
ufually come in the prime of life, they muft raife
the proportion of *inhabitants* to the *deaths*, and
alfo of *births* and *weddings* to the *burials*, higher
than they would otherwife be. However, exclufive of this confideration, there is good reafon to
believe that Manchefter is more healthy now
than formerly. The new ftreets are wide and
fpacious, the poor have larger and more com-
modious dwellings, and the increafe of trade
affords them better clothing and diet than they
before enjoyed. I may add too, that the late
improvements in medicine have been highly
favourable to the prefervation of life. The cool
regimen in fevers, and in the fmall-pox; the free
admiffion of air; attention to cleanlinefs; and the
general ufe of antifeptic remedies and diet, have
certainly mitigated the violence, and leffened the
mortality of fome of the moft dangerous and
malignant diftempers to which mankind are
incident. The ulcerous fore throat, which prevailed here in the year 1770, is the only epidemic
which has appeared in Manchefter, with any fatal
degree of violence, for many years. Miliary
fevers, which were formerly frequent in this town
and neighbourhood, now rarely occur; and if I
may judge from my own experience, the natural
fmall-pox (for inoculation is not much practifed
here) carries off a fmaller proportion of thofe

who

who are attacked by it, than is commonly fuppofed. Puerperal difeafes alfo decreafe every
year amongft us, by the judicious method of
treating women in child-bed: and as nature is
now more confulted in the management of infants, it is reafonable to fuppofe that this muft be
favourable to their health and prefervation.

But it muft be acknowledged that large towns
are injurious to population; and the advantages
I have enumerated, which in hamlets or country
villages would have operated with full force to
the benefit of mankind, have only ferved to check
the deftructive tendency of the accumulation of
inhabitants in Manchefter. In the Pais de Vaud,
a diftrict of the province of Bern in Switzerland,
and in a country parifh in Brandenburgh, 1 in 45
of the inhabitants die annually; and at Stoke
Damarell in Devonfhire, 1 in 54 (e): whereas in
this town the yearly mortality appears to be 1 in
28; in Leverpool 1 in 27; and in London 1 in
21. Half the children who are born in Manchefter die under five years old; and the proportion which the births bear to the number of
inhabitants who attain the age of 80, is as 30 to 1.
Difeafes are moft frequent and fatal here in the
months of January, February, and March; and

(e) See the Treatife before referred to, on Reverfionary
Payments, by my learned friend Dr. Price.

leaft

leaft fo in July, Auguft, and September. The
mortality of thefe two feafons is as 11 to 8; and
of the firft fix months of the year compared with
the laft fix months, as 7 to 6.

In April, 1773, feveral gentlemen, from motives of curiofity, undertook an enumeration of
the people of BOLTON, a manufacturing town
about twelve miles diftant from Manchefter.
The houfes were found to be 946; the males
2159; the females 2392; and perfons aged
feventy years and upwards, 74. To thefe numbers 17 muft be added, which by a miftake
were not claffed under either denomination. The
inhabitants of Bolton therefore amount to
4568; the number of individuals to a houfe is
4 .8; and about a fixtieth part of the people
have attained the age of feventy.

LITTLE BOLTON, a fuburb of Bolton, including
the manor, and extending into the country as far
as the inhabitants are fubject to *fuit* and *fervice*,
contains 232 houfes; 771 individuals; 361
males; 410 females; and 15 perfons aged
feventy years and upwards. From this account
it appears that the inhabitants are 3 .3 to a houfe;
and that 1 in 51 has reached the age of feventy.
The difference in thefe proportions between a
fmall *town*, and a *country manor* contiguous to it,
is worthy of obfervation.

Mr.

Mr. Fletcher has favoured me with an enumeration of the people of Bury, which he has just executed with great care. The town contains 463 houses; 464 families; and 2090 inhabitants. Each house and family therefore consists of 4½ individuals. Bury is situated nine miles from Manchester, and is enriched by a branch of the woollen manufactory.

At Altringham, a market town in Cheshire, which has no manufactory, the number of houses, according to an exact survey made in July, 1772, was 248; of inhabitants 1029, or 4¼ to a house. An enumeration of the people of this town was made about twenty years ago, at which time they amounted very nearly to 1000.

The following is a comparative view of the state of population, the duration of life, and the mortality of the several seasons of the year, &c. in Eastham, and Royton, two country places widely different from each other in climate, situation, and in the occupation of their inhabitants.

The parish of Eastham lies in Wirral, one of the hundreds into which Cheshire is divided, and is extended along the banks of the river Mersey, a few miles distant from the Irish sea. The people are most of them farmers; though some are fishermen, and others are employed in the ferry to Leverpool.

ROYTON

Royton is a chapelry, fituated ten miles eaft-ward of Manchefter, under the great chain of mountains which divides Lancafhire and York-fhire. The inhabitants are employed chiefly in the cotton and linen manufactory; a few of them are farmers; and fome I believe work in the coal pits, with which this country abounds.

I am indebted to my learned friend the Rev. Mr. Travis, Vicar of Eaftham, for the furvey of his own parifh, which he undertook at my defire, and executed himfelf; and alfo for that of Royton, which was made by his uncle, the wor-thy and refpectable clergyman of that chapelry.

JANUARY 1st, 1772, the number of inhabitants in the chapelry of Royton were found to be 1105.

The number of inhabitants in the parish of Eastham, 912.

The number of persons *in a house*, in the chapelry of Royton is somewhat more than - - - 5 7.

The number of ditto, in the parish of Eastham, - - - exactly - 5.

The number of persons *in a family*, in the former, on an average, - - about - 4 3/4.

The number of ditto, - in the latter, - - - more than - 4 1/2.

The proportion of males to females, in Royton, - - nearly as - 53 to 56.

The proportion of ditto, - in Eastham, - - nearly as - 54 1/2 to 56.

The widows to the widowers, - in Royton, - - as - - 3 1/3 to 1.

The widows ditto, - in Eastham, - - as - - 3 to 2 1/2.

The number of births in Royton (on an average of 3 years) 42. } Proportion between males and females as 13 to 11.

The number of ditto, - in Eastham ditto, 34. } Proportion between ditto, as 18 to 16.

N. B. These proportions for 7 years.

The number of births in Royton to the number of married inhabitants, as (very nearly) 1 child to 5 married couples.

The number of do. in Eastham to ditto, - - as (somewhat more than) 1 child to 4 married couples.

The number of births in Royton to the whole number of inhabitants, - - as - - 1 to 26 1/3.

The number of do. in Eastham to ditto, - - as - - 1 to 26 4/5.

The number of married persons in Royton to the number of unmarried persons above 15, - as - - 8 to 5.

The number of ditto, - in Eastham to the number of - ditto, - ditto, - nearly as 6 to 5.

The number of burials in Royton (on an average of 3 years) 21. } Proportion between males and females as 13 to 10.

The number of ditto in Eastham - ditto - 26. } Proportion between - ditto - as 14 to 12.

The number of burials in Royton to the number of all the inhabitants, - as - 1 to 52.

The number of ditto in Eastham to - ditto, - - - as - 1 to 35.

The number of children dying under 3 yrs. old to the number of children born in Royton (on an average of 3 yrs.) as 1 to 7.

The number of children - ditto - to - ditto - in Eastham - - as 1 to 17.

Persons alive in Royton under 3 years old Jan. 1, 1772, 129; dead under 3 years old, average of 3 years, 6, or 1 of 21¼.

Ditto in Eastham - - - 100; - - - dead 2, or 1 of 50.

Persons alive in Royton under 15 years old Jan. 1, 1772, 450; dead under 15 years old, average of 3 years, 11, or 1 of 41.

Ditto in Eastham - - - 329; - - - dead 4, or 1 of 82.

Persons alive in Royton between 15 and 30 years old Jan. 1, 1772, 333; dead before 1773 of these 5, or 1 of 66¼.

Ditto in Eastham - - - 199; - dead 5, or 1 of 40.

Persons alive in Royton from 30 to 40 years old ditto, 96; dead before 1773 of these on an average, 2, or 1 of 48.

Ditto in Eastham - - - 124; - dead 4, or 1 of 31.

Persons alive in Royton from 40 to 50 years old ditto, 98; dead before 1773 of these on an average, 2, or 1 of 49.

Ditto in Eastham - - - 83; dead before 1773 of these - 3, or 1 of 28.

Persons alive in Royton from 50 to 60 years old ditto, 61; dead before 1773 of these - 1¼, or 1 of 45.

Ditto in Eastham - - - 64; dead before 1773 of these - 2, or 1 of 32.

Perfons alive in Royton from 60 to 70 years old ditto, 49; dead before 1773 of these -   -   1⅓, or 1 of 36.
Ditto   in Eastham   -   -   54; dead before 1773 of these -   -   1⅓, or 1 of 40.
Perfons alive in Royton from 70 to 80, Jan. 1, 1772, 10 } above 70 years, 18 { dead before 1773, on an } 1 of 18.
80 to 90,   ditto,   8 } average of 3 years,
Perfons alive in Eastham from 70 to 80, ditto, 34 } above 70 years, 39 { dead before 1773, on an } 1 of 21.
80 to 90,   ditto,   5 } average of 3 years,

(f)

THE mortality of the seasons at Royton and Eastham, for the last seven years, has been as follows:

		ROYTON.	EASTHAM.
January,	February, March,	39	56
April,	May, June,	31	34
July,	August, September,	31	45
October,	November, December,	18	53
		119	188

(f) THE averages here adopted may, in some instances, seem to be too small; but Mr. Travis assures me, that through a series of fifteen successive years, the marriages, births, and deaths at Eastham, do not vary, in any degree worth remarking, from the foregoing table.

Of all the months in the year fingly taken, October is the moft, and April the leaft fatal to the inhabitants of Eaftham. Whereas the three laft months of the year appear to be the moft healthful at Royton; although a very large quantity of rain ufually falls there during this feafon. For the wind at this time being generally wefterly, the clouds are intercepted by the high mountains, and difcharge themfelves in frequent and heavy fhowers. At Townley, which is fituated under the fame chain of hills, and is not very far diftant from Royton, 42 inches of rain fall at a medium, every year. The quantity of rain at Manchefter, which is farther removed from the mountains, is about 33 inches *communibus annis (g)*. It has been obferved by a very ufeful writer, that the *moift feafons* in Great Britain and Ireland are more remarkably free from epidemic difeafes, than the dry ones; and that ftorms, the ufual concomitants of rain, are attended with more health and lefs ficknefs than calm weather, probably becaufe they diffipate the vapours, which by ftagnation might prove an occafion of various diftem-

---

(g) The rain-gauge at Townley appears to have been placed on the top of the houfe; whereas, at Manchefter, this inftrument was very near the ground. It is evident, therefore, that the difparity muft be eftimated at much more than nine inches.

pers

pers *(h)*. I fhall not prefume to determine, that thefe obfervations account for the fuperior healthinefs of the laft months of the year at Royton; but they certainly fhould remove the prejudice which is too generally entertained againft the wetnefs of the climate in Lancafhire, and other weftern counties of England. For the bounties of Providence are difpenfed with an equal, as well as with a liberal hand. And if we, in this part of the ifland, enjoy lefs funfhine than our neighbours, we have milder winters, and fummers tempered with more refrefhing fhowers, to balance the inconvenience.

THE REV. Mr. Bolton, a very worthy diffenting clergyman at MONTON, a few miles from Manchefter, has at my requeft, made an enumeration of his people, with a retrofpective view of the births and deaths amongft them during the laft ten years. By this furvey, his congregation, including fervants, confifts of 196 males; 190 females; 97 families; 60 married perfons; 14 widowers; 13 widows; 142 under 15 years of age; and 64 above 50. The deaths during ten years have been 57, and the births 138. Hence it appears, that of this fociety 1 in 6 has attained the age of 50; that the births are more than double the burials;

(h) Rutty's Chronological Hiftory of Weather.

and

and that only 1 in 68, at a medium, dies every year. The laſt circumſtance is ſomewhat extraordinary; but to remove all doubts concerning the accuracy of his enumeration, Mr. Bolton, with the moſt obliging aſſiduity, has repeated it twice. And he has derived his information not only from the regiſter of his chapel, but alſo from the private records, or deliberate recollection of every family in his congregation. The *ſituation* of Monton appears to be rather unfavourable to health, from the vicinity of a large moſs; but the people are moſt of them farmers, and are remarkable for their diligence and ſobriety. The long life which they enjoy affords a ſtriking and pleaſing proof of the great advantages of temperance; and confirms a curious obſervation of M. Muret, who examined the regiſter of mortality in one town, to mark thoſe whoſe deaths might be imputed to *exceſs*. The number of theſe he found ſo great, as led him to believe that *drunkenneſs* is more deſtructive to mankind than pleuriſies, fevers, or the moſt malignant diſtempers.

A u g. 16, 1773.

FARTHER

FURTHER OBSERVATIONS

ON THE

STATE *of* POPULATION *in* MANCHESTER, *and
other* ADJACENT PLACES.

THE number of inhabitants and progrefs
of population in the kingdom; the increafe or
decreafe of certain difeafes; the comparative
healthinefs of different fituations, climates, and
feafons; and the influence of particular trades
and manufactures on the duration of life, are
fubjects of the higheft importance to the com-
munity; and equally interefting to the ftatefman,
the philofopher, and the phyfician.

" I have fomewhere read," fays Dr. Franklin
(in the remarks on my former paper with which
he has lately favoured me) " that in China an
" account is yearly taken of the number of
" people; and of the quantities of provifion pro-
" duced.   This account is tranfmitted to the
" Emperor, whofe minifters can thence fore-
" fee a fcarcity likely to happen in any province,
" and from what province it can beft be fupplied
" in good time *(a)*. To facilitate the collect-
" ing of this account, and prevent the neceffity

(a) CHINA, like all other countries that fubfift chiefly
upon rice, is fubject to frequent famines. *Montefquieu.*

" of entering houfes, and fpending time in afk-
" ing and anfwering queftions, each houfe is
" furnifhed with a little board, to be hung with-
" out the door during a certain time each
" year; on which board are marked certain
" words, againft which the inhabitant is to
" mark *number* or *quantity*, fomewhat in this
" manner :

MEN

WOMEN

CHILDREN

RICE *or* WHEAT

FLESH, &c.

" ALL under fixteen are accounted children,
" and all above, men and women. Any other
" particulars, which the government defires in-
" formation of, are occafionally marked on the fame
" boards. Thus the officers appointed to col-
" lect the accounts in each diftrict, have only to
" pafs before the doors, and enter into their
" book what they find marked on the board,
" without giving the leaft trouble to the family.
" There is a penalty on marking falfely; and as
" neighbours muft know nearly the truth of each
" other's account, they dare not expofe them-
" felves, by a falfe one, to each other's accufation.
                                        " Perhaps

" Perhaps fuch a regulation is fcarcely practica-
" ble with us."

But an enumeration of the people of England,
fimilar to that lately executed at Manchefter,
would not be fo difficult an undertaking, as may
at the firft view be imagined.   And if accurate,
and comprehenfive Bills of Mortality were univerfally eftablifhed, they would admirably coin-
cide with the views of fuch inquiries, and give
precifion and certainty to the conclufions deduced
from them (b).

From the populoufnefs of this neighbourhood,
it may perhaps be fuppofed, that a great number
of burials are brought from the country to the
collegiate and other churches in Manchefter, and
that this circumftance is likely to create uncertainty and error in the calculations made from
the parochial regifter of deaths.   But it appears,
from the beft information I can collect, that the
number of fuch burials is not confiderable; and
that they are pretty exactly balanced by thofe
which are carried out of Manchefter to the
neighbouring epifcopal or diffenting chapels.
This fact admits of an eafy and fatisfactory

(b) See Propofals for eftablifhing accurate Bills of
Mortality in Manchefter, vol. I. p. 428.   Thefe Propofals
have been adopted, and, with a few variations, carried into
execution by Dr. Haygarth at Chefter, Dr. Dobfon at
Leverpool, and by Mr. John Aikin at Warrington.

explanation, were it neceſſary to trouble the reader with it.

It is remarked, in the former paper, that wet ſeaſons are generally more free from epidemic diſeaſes than dry ones, and the Bills of Mortality at Mancheſter *ſeem* to confirm the obſervation: It appears at leaſt from the following table, that the year 1766, remarkable in this climate for the ſmall quantity of rain which fell during the courſe of it, was more fatal than any of the reſt. And the proportion of deaths will be deemed greater, when it is recollected, that the town contained at that time fewer inhabitants probably, by two thouſand, than it does at preſent. For the rapid increaſe of Mancheſter commenced about the year 1765, after the concluſion of the laſt war.

Year.	Quantity of Rain at Mancheſter. Inches.	Deaths at Mancheſter.
1765	31. 378	723
1766	25. 762	1019
1767	29. 186	690
1768	40. 526	867
1769	32. 514	788
1770	39. 363	988
1771 from Jan. 1. to June 1.	6. 8 *(c)*	

THIS

(c) This account of the quantity of rain, was communicated to me by George Lloyd, Eſq. F. R. S. The obſervations

THIS table, it muft be acknowledged, does not comprehend a fufficient length of time to

tions were made at his feat, about a mile diftant from the centre of Manchefter, and were continued only till June 1771.

THE following is an abridged view of a meteorological regifter, which I kept, with great exactnefs, during the years 1774 and 1775.

Months.	1774. Thermometer. Two o'Clock P. M.		Days.	
	Higheft.	Loweft.	Rainy.	Dry.
Jan. Feb. March,	56.	28.	25.	65.
April, May, June,	72.	45.	55.	36.
July, Aug. Sept.	75.	53.	66.	26.
Oct. Nov. Dec.	60.	30.	43.	49.
Mean heat 52,25.			189.	176.

Months.	1775.			
Jan. Feb. March,	54.	30.	61.	29.
April, May, June,	78.	51.	42.	49.
July, Aug. Sept.	74.	48.	62.	30.
Oct. Nov. Dec.	64.	32.	50.	28.
Mean heat 55,7			215.	136.

N. B. IN 1775, fourteen days are omitted, no account being taken.

THE thermometer was made by Dollond, and graduated according to the fcale of Fahrenheit. It was placed in the open air, and in a northern expofure. The column of rainy days exprefles the *leaft*, as well as the *greateft* quantity of rain; the column of days includes only thofe days, in which not a fingle fhower was noticed. The day comprehends twenty-four hours.

C 3   admit

admit of any very accurate or incontrovertible conclusions. And the influence of other causes of disease, which have little or no relation to the state of the atmosphere, together with the irregularity which necessarily occurs in the annual increase of a large manufacturing town, may be regarded as farther sources of fallacy and uncertainty. It is therefore with diffidence I observe, that though wet seasons are less mortal than long continued droughts, yet the rainy years 1768 and 1770 proved extremely sickly and fatal. And those years are probably most unfavourable to health, in which heavy rains fall about the beginning of summer, and are succeeded by great and uninterrupted heats. For the earth being thus drenched with moisture, and the low lands overflowed with water, the exhalations become constant, copious, and often putrid.

Joan Leo in his history of Africa relates, that if heavy rains fall in that country during the months of July and August, the plague usually breaks out the September following *(d)*. But in European climates, it is well remarked by Sir John Pringle, that frequent showers in summer cool the air, check the excess of vapour, dilute and refresh the corrupted waters,

(d) Hist. Africæ, lib. I. cap. 10.

and precipitate the noxious effluvia which float in the atmofphere *(e)*. And it appears, from a variety of obfervations which I have collected, that October, November, and December are generally very healthy, although the moft rainy months in the year. I fhall fubjoin a table which will fet this point in the cleareft light; and at the fame time fhew the comparative mortality of the different feafons at Middleton, Bowden, Chowbent, Difhley, Middlewich, Richmond, and Manchefter. *(f)*

(e) See Sir John Pringle on the Difeafes of the Army, p. 5, edit. fourth.

(f) Extract of a letter from Dr. Farr, dated April 13, 1782.

" BEFORE I left the Briftol Infirmary, I took an ac-
" count of all the difeafes which occurred in it for a number
" of years ; and as all acute cafes are admitted, it is, in
" general, an epitome of the ftate of difeafes in the town.
" I have fent you an account for three years, during which
" time I kept a regifter of the rain."

	1775	1776	1777
Synochus - - -	166	95	137
Typhus - - -	35	21	33
Intermittents - -	16	14	4
Pleurifies and Peripneumonies	20	43	25
Inflammations - -	8	15	18
Acute Rheumatifm - -	52	66	64
	297	254	281
Rain. Inches, - -	38,597,	28,554,	23,369

A TABLE

A TABLE shewing the comparative MORTALITY of the different SEASONS of the YEAR.

	Middleton from 1663 to 1673. Ten years.	Middleton from 1763 to 1773. Ten years.	Bowden from 1663 to 1673. Ten years.	Bowden from 1763 to 1773. Ten years.	Manchester from 1766 to 1774.* Eight years.
January, February, March,	117.	265.	179.	259.	1538.
April, May, June,	99.	291.	139.	300.	1366.
July, August, September,	79.	215.	114.	209.	957.
October, November, December.	72.	222.	127.	207.	1339.

* This account is taken from the register of the collegiate or parish church only.

Chowbent

	Chowbent from 1767 to 1773. Six years.	Dishley from 1763 to 1773. Ten years.	Middlewich from 1768 to 1773. Five years.	Richmond from 1764 to 1774. Ten years.	Rochdale from 1760 to 1773. Thirteen years.
January, February, March,	71.	64.	67.	170.	1533.
April, May, June,	37.	78.	55.	156.	1336.
July, August, September,	28.	51.	59.	172.	1077.
October, November, December.	33.	43.	69.	144.	1239.
Total.					

Total.	Jan.	Feb.	March,	4263.
	April,	May,	June,	3857.
	July,	Aug.	Sep.	2961.
	Oct.	Nov.	Dec.	3495.

THERE is a confiderable diverfity in the fituation of thefe places. Middleton lies fix miles north eaft of Manchefter, not far from the great chain of mountains which divides Lancafhire and Yorkfhire; and about thirty-fix miles from the fea.

BOWDEN is ten miles to the fouth weft of Manchefter, and thirty-five miles from the fea. It is an elevated fituation, in a level country; and at a great diftance from any hills.

CHOWBENT is ten miles weftward of Manchefter, and twenty five miles diftant from the fea. It is in a low and flat fituation, and near a very extenfive morafs.

DISHLEY is in that part of Chefhire, which borders on the peak of Derbyfhire. It is a mountainous fituation, thirteen miles fouth eaft of Manchefter, and fifty miles from the fea.

MIDDLEWICH is twenty eight miles fouthward of Manchefter, and about forty miles from the fea. It is furrounded by a well cultivated and level country.

RICHMOND is a confiderable market town in the north riding of Yorkfhire, about forty miles
diftant

diftant from the German ocean.   It ftands on
an eminence, which terminates a long continued range of mountains.   The country below
is an extenfive, rich, and well cultivated plain.

THE obfervations of Dr. Franklin on the
fubject of moifture will, I doubt not, be very
acceptable to the medical reader, although he
may not entirely acquiefce in the opinion of this
excellent philofopher.   I fhall therefore give a
farther quotation from the letter before referred
to.   " The gentry of England are remarkably
" afraid of moifture, and of air.   But feamen,
" who live in perpetually moift air, are always
" healthy if they have good provifions.   The
" inhabitants of Bermudas, St. Helen, and other
" iflands far from continents, furrounded with
" rocks, againft which the waves continually
" dafhing fill the air with fpray and vapour, and
" where no wind can arife that does not pafs
" over much fea, and of courfe bring much
" moifture, are remarkably healthy.   And I
" have long thought, mere moift air has no ill
" effect on the conftitution; though air impreg-
" nated with vapours from putrid marfhes is
" found pernicious, not from its moifture, but
" putridity.   It feems ftrange that a man, whofe
" body is compofed in great part of moift fluids,
" whofe blood and juices are fo watery, who can
" fwallow quantities of water and fmall beer
" daily

" daily, without inconvenience, fhould fancy that
" a little more or lefs moifture in the air fhould
" be of fuch importance. But we abound in
" abfurdity and inconfiftency."

In the former paper, I gave a ftriking example of the great advantages of diligence and
fobriety, in *the length of days* which the people of
Monton enjoy. Such an inftance, though a fingle one, affords the moft animating leffon of
morality; and I can enforce it by farther proofs.

The Rev. Mr. Harrop has favoured me with
an account of the people who attend divine
fervice in the chapel at Hale, near Altringham,
which he has lately taken, with a retrofpect of the
births and deaths amongft them during the laft
feven years. The fociety is compofed of 140
males, 136 females, 92 married perfons, 8
widowers, 12 widows, 105 under fifteen years of
age, and 41 above fifty. The deaths during
feven years have been 28, and the births 68.
It appears from this enumeration, that only one
in 69 of the people, who are moft of them farmers, dies annually. Hale is a low fituation,
and the foil is clayey.

The congregration belonging to the chapel at
Horwich confifts of 305 individuals, viz. 149
males, and 156 females, 94 married perfons, and
9 widowers, 8 widows, 127 under fifteen years of
age, and 50 above fifty. The births for the laft
feven

feven years have amounted to 101, and the deaths to 32. Hence the yearly proportion of deaths to the inhabitants is as 1 to 66. Horwich is between Bolton and Chorley, the country is mountainous, and the people are compofed almoft equally of farmers and manufacturers. I am obliged to the Rev. Mr. Evans for this account.

THE Rev. Mr. Smalley of Darwen, three miles from Blackburn in Lancafhire, has tranf-mitted to me the following furvey of his congre-gation. It confifts of 1850 individuals; 900 males; 950 females; 640 married perfons; 30 widowers; 48 widows; 737 perfons under the age of fifteen, and 218 above fifty. During the laft feven years the deaths have amounted to 233; and the births to 508. The annual pro-portion of deaths therefore is 1 in 56; and the births are to the number of inhabitants nearly as 1 to 25 .5. Darwen is a country diftrict, bleak and elevated in its fituation, furrounded by moors, and ill cultivated. The inhabitants are chiefly employed in the cotton manufactory.

A CLERGYMAN in the peak of Derbyfhire has, at my defire, undertaken an enumeration of the people of Edale, a fertile valley in that part of the county, inhabited by a fober and induftrious race of farmers. But I have not yet received a particular account of the furvey; and have only been

been informed, that 1 in 59 of the inhabitants dies annually, on an average of ten years.

THE principles and manners of the Quakers, though often made the subjects of illiberal censure and ridicule, may probably afford them advantages, with respect to the duration of life, over other bodies of men. The diligence, cleanliness, temperance and compofure of mind, by which the members of this fociety are in general diftinguifhed, may reafonably be fuppofed to contribute to health and longevity: And as there are no perfons among them in abject poverty, and few immoderately rich, this more equal diftribution of property muft leffen the fources of difeafe, and furnifh every individual under it with the neceffary means of relief. Thefe confiderations excited my curiofity to know the proportion of deaths amongft the Quakers in Manchefter; and I have been gratified by Mr. Routh, in the moft obliging manner, with the following information. The fociety confifts of 81 males; and 84 females; 54 married perfons; 9 widowers; 7 widows; and 48 perfons under fifteen years of age. The births during the laft feven years have amounted to 34; and the burials to 47. About 1 therefore in 24.6 of the Quakers in Manchefter dies annually; whereas the proportion of deaths amongft the inhabitants of the town at large

is

is as 1 to 28. If no allowance be made for
the temporary and accidental irregularities which
may occur in a fingle and fmall body of men,
when the average of a few years has only been
taken, a conclufion directly contrary to what
I have prefuppofed, will be drawn from this
fact. And perhaps it will be urged, that the
want of vivacity in the people of this fect, and
the fedentary lives of their females, are caufes
which fhorten the period of their exiftence,
and counterbalance the advantages from cleanlinefs and fobriety, which they enjoy. But the
reader will entertain a different opinion concerning this point, when he is informed, that
the Quakers here have had few or no acceffions
to their number, by fupplies from other places,
during the laft feven years. This muft confiderably increafe their proportional mortality, for
reafons which have been before affigned; and
is the true caufe, why the deaths amongft them
fo much exceed the births. Were it not for
new fettlers in the prime of life, who annually
pour into Manchefter, it is probable that more
than 1 in 25 of its inhabitants would die annually. So baleful is the influence of large towns
on the duration of life; and fo juftly are they
ftiled, by a writer of the moft diftinguifhed abi-
lities, the *graves* of mankind *(g)* !

(g) Dr. Price.   T H E

THE Rev. Mr. Barnes, whom I cannot mention without expreffions of efteem and friend-fhip, made a furvey in September, 1773, of the people belonging to the new chapel at Cockey Moor, near Bolton, the particulars of which are as follow :

Houfes	150.
Families	154.
Males	320.
Females	391.
Married perfons	248.
Widowers	10.
Widows	27.
Under fifteen	252.
Above fifty	99.
Births in five years	125.
Deaths in feven years	114.
Total number of people	711.

THE married perfons in this fociety are therefore to the fingle as 1 to 1 .867 ; the widows are nearly treble the number of widowers ; a feventh part of the people have attained the age of fifty, and thofe under fifteen exceed one third of the whole congregation. The average number of births is 25 every year, and of deaths $16\frac{2}{7}$; fo that the former are to the latter, in the proportion of fomewhat more than 5 to 3 ; and 1 per-

fon

fon in about 44 dies annually. It fhould be remarked, that the number of deaths in this period was confiderably increafed by the uncommon fatality of the fmall-pox in the year 1770. Cockey Moor is furrounded by a cold, wet, and barren country; the inhabitants are farmers and manufacturers.

THE congregation belonging to the chapel at Chowbent confifts of 1160 perfons, viz. 554 males; 606 females; 173 males, and 150 females under 10 years of age; 83 males, and 91 females above fifty; 6 males, and 4 females above eighty; 199 married couples; 26 widowers; and 43 widows. The baptifms during fix years (wanting fix weeks) have amounted to 293; and the deaths to 169. About 1 therefore in 41 .2 of this fociety dies annually. This furvey was made in November, 1773, by the Rev. Mr. Mercer. The people of Chowbent are employed chiefly in the manufactories of cotton, linen, and iron.

AT Ackworth, near Ferry-bridge in the county of York, the chriftenings and burials for ten years, viz. from March 25th 1757, to March 25th 1767, have been as follow:

CHRISTENINGS.		BURIALS.	
Males	104.	Males.	79.
Females	108.	Females	77.
Total	212.	Total	156.

Of this number have died,

	Males.	Females.	Total.
Under 2 years old	18	13	31
Between 2 and 5	9	7	16
5 and 10	4	1	5
10 and 20	2	2	4
20 and 30	7	5	12
30 and 40	3	8	11
40 and 50	2	4	6
50 and 60	11	3	14
60 and 70	13	13	26
70 and 80	7	14	21
80 and 90	3	6	9
90 and 100	0	1	1
Of all ages in ten years	79	77	156

DISEASES.	Males.	Females.	Total.
Child-bed	0	2	2
Chincough	0	2	2
Confumption	23	15	38
Diabetes	1	0	1
Fever	12	11	23
Infants	7	6	13
Meafles	0	2	2
Old Age	11	19	30
Small Pox	7	6	13
Dyfentery	1	1	2
Dropfy	0	3	3
Apoplexy	2	1	3

In

In this parish there are,

184 Houfes, eleven of which are uninhabited.

728 Perfons, of the following ages, viz.

	Males.	Females.	Total.
Under 2 Years old	31	25	56
Between 2 and 5	32	36	68
5 and 10	34	38	72
10 and 20	50	51	101
20 and 30	44	63	107
30 and 40	61	62	123
40 and 50	31	38	69
50 and 60	28	32	60
60 and 70	20	28	48
70 and 80	7	10	17
80 and 90	2	4	6
90 and 100	0	1	1
Of all ages — Total	340	388	

THIS account of Ackworth was lately tranf-
mitted to my friend Mr. White, by the Rev.
Dr. Lee, Rector of the parifh. It appears
that 1 in 46 .6 of the inhabitants dies yearly;
and that the proportion of perfons to each tenanted houfe is 4 ¹⁄₅. Amongft the males under
2 years of age, the number of deaths exceeds,
by a third, thofe amongft the females; and 43
women and only 29 men have attained the age

D 2   of

of fixty and upwards.   Thefe facts (and I could
adduce many fimilar ones)   confirm a curious
remark lately advanced by Dr. Price, that the
life of males is more frail than that of females.

I SHALL conclude this Paper with a Table
deduced from the preceding obfervations.

FEB. 1ft, 1774.

A TABLE

A TABLE shewing the PROPORTION of INHABITANTS *dying annually* in several different Places.

MANCHESTER.	LEVERPOOL.	CHOWBENT.	EASTHAM.	COCKEY.	ROYTON.
1. in 28.	1. in 27 .7.	1. in 41.	1. in 35.	1. in 44.	1. in 52.
DARWEN.	EDALE.	ACKWORTH.	HORWICH.	HALE.	MONTON.
1. in 56.	1. in 59.	1. in 47.	1. in 66.	1. in 69.	1. in 68.

OBSERVATIONS

ON THE ,

STATE *of* POPULATION *in* MANCHESTER, *and other* ADJACENT PLACES, *concluded.*

A VERY accurate furvey was completed laft year of the towns of Manchefter and Salford, with their refpective townfhips. This fpring an enumeration, equally exact and comprehenfive, has been made of the whole parifh of Manchefter; which contains thirty-one townfhips (exclufive of the two above-mentioned) in the compafs of lefs than fixty fquare miles. The reader is here prefented with the particulars of this enumeration.

Tenanted houfes	2371.
Families	2525.
Inhabitants	13,786.
Males	6942.
Females	6844.
Married	4319.
Widowers	232.
Widows	315.
Under fifteen	5545.
Above fifty	1762.
Above fixty	470.

Above

Above seventy	261.
Above eighty	87.
Male lodgers	68.
Female lodgers	51.
Empty houses	41.

THE number of persons to a house, in the parish of Manchester, is therefore nearly $5\frac{4}{5}$; of individuals to a family about $5\frac{1}{2}$; and $\frac{1}{5}$th of the inhabitants have attained the age of fifty. It is unnecessary to point out the difference in the proportions between the *town* and adjacent *country*, as it will appear sufficiently obvious, by comparing this account with that of Manchester. The whole number of inhabitants in the town, township, and parish of Manchester, amounts to 42937.

AT the close of 1772, an account was collected from every country chapel, both Episcopal and Dissenting, in the parish, of the baptisms and burials of that year. The former were found to amount to 401; the latter to 246; and there is a presumption, that this is nearly the annual proportion of deaths in the parish of Manchester, exclusive of the town and township. For the number of burials in the whole parish was, in the same year, exactly 1200; and it has been shewn, that the deaths in the town of Manchester are, one year with another,

958.

958. This sum being subtracted from 1200, leaves a remainder (242) for the country, very nearly equal to 246.   And if 13786, the number of people in the parish, be divided by 246, it will appear that only one in 56 of the inhabitants dies annually; whilst the yearly mortality in Manchester is as 1 to 28.   Such a striking disparity in the healthiness of a large town, and of the country which surrounds it, granting it to be less than has been supposed, will scarcely be credited by those, who have paid no attention to inquiries of this nature.   And it must afford matter of astonishment even to the physician and philosopher, when he reflects, that the inhabitants of both live in the same climate, carry on the same manufactures, and are chiefly supplied with provisions from the same market. But his surprise will give place to concern and regret, when he observes the havoc produced in every large town by luxury, irregularity, and intemperance (a); the numbers that fall annual

(a) There are at this time, in Manchester, no less than 193 licensed houses for retailing spirituous and other liquors; and 64 in the other townships of the parish.   At Birmingham, the number of public houses is still greater than at Manchester.   A very ingenious friend of mine in that place has computed, that the quantity of malt consumed there in the public houses, requires for its growth, a compass of land which would be sufficient for the support of 20,000 men.

victims

victims to the contagious diftempers, which
never ceafe to prevail ; and the pernicious influence of confinement, uncleanlinefs, and foul
air on the duration of life *(b)*.

> Ye who amid this feverifh world would wear
> A body free of pain, of cares a mind ;
> Fly the rank city, fhun its turbid air ;
> Breathe not the chaos of eternal fmoke
> And volatile corruption, from the dead,
> The dying, fickening, and the living world
> Exhaled, to fully heaven's tranfparent dome
> With dim mortality.
>
> *Armftrong on Health*, Book I.

GREAT towns are in a peculiar degree fatal
to children. Half of all that are born in
London die under two, and in Manchefter under
five years of age ; whereas at Royton, a country
townfhip not far diftant from Manchefter, the
number of children dying under the age of three
years, is to the number of children born only as
1 to 7 : and at Eaftham, a parifh in Chefhire
inhabited by farmers, the proportion is confiderably lefs.

IT is a common, but injurious practice, in manufacturing countries, to confine children, before

---

(b) THE Rev. Dr. Tucker, Dean of Gloucefter, informs
me, " That were it not for the daily arrival of recruits from
" the country, his parifh (St. Stephens, in Briftol) and in-
" deed Briftol in general, would be left in a century without
" an inhabitant ; unlefs the people fhould betake themfelves
" to better courfes."

they

they have attained a fufficient degree of ftrength, to fedentary employments, in places where they breathe a putrid air, and are debarred the free ufe of their limbs. The effect of this confinement, fays an able writer, is either to cut them off early in life, or to render their conftitutions feeble and fickly. But the love of money ftifles the feelings of humanity, and even makes men blind to the very intereft they fo anxioufly purfue. The fame principle of found policy, which induces them to fpare their horfes and cattle, till they arrive at a due fize and vigour, fhould determine them to grant a proportionable refpite to their children *(c)*. And this obfervation may, perhaps, be extended to the untimely culture of the mind. For too early an application to ftudy impairs the faculties, injures the conftitution, and hurts the temper by frequent contradiction. Almoft as foon as a boy has acquired the powers of fpeech, he is fhut up many hours every day in a noifome fchool, fecluded from the benefit of exercife and the refrefhment of the open air, and tied down to the fevere drudgery of learning what ferves only, at fuch a period of life, to overcharge his me-mory, and to deftroy his native cheerfulnefs of difpofition. Thus the age of gaiety (to ufe the

(c) See Dr. Gregory's Comparative View of the State and Faculties of Man, &c.

words

words of the elegant writer before referred to) is
spent in the midst of tears, punishments, and
slavery; and this to answer no other end but to
make a child a man, some years before nature
intended he should be one.

THE Rev. Mr. Harrison of Chapel in le Frith
has made a survey, at my request, of the inhabitants of Chinley, Brownside, and Bugsworth;
three hamlets contiguous to each other, in the
parish of Glossop, and peak of Derbyshire.
They are four statute miles in length, and three
in breadth; and contain 301 males; 310 females;
200 married persons; 15 widowers; 18 widows;
234 persons under fifteen years of age; 121
above fifty; and 9 who have attained the age of
eighty. This enumeration was finished in September, 1773.

I HAVE been furnished by the Rev. Mr.
Asheton, Rector of Middleton near Manchester,
with an account of the births, deaths, and marriages in his parish, during ten corresponding
years of the last, and of the present century.
From 1663 to 1672 inclusive, the deaths were,
males 180, females 187; the births, males 200,
females 188; the marriages 121.

THE births therefore, during ten years, only
exceeded the deaths in number 21; and the
average number of births to each marriage, was
as 3¼ to 1.

From 1763 to 1772 inclusive, the deaths were, 499 males, 494 females; the christenings, 802 males, 768 females; the marriages 330. The baptisms therefore, during this period, exceeded the deaths 577, that is, near 58 annually. And if no allowance be made for illegitimate births (which, I believe, in this parish are not numerous, and can no where be supposed equal to one fourth of all that are born) each marriage has produced $4\frac{3}{4}$ children.

It is curious to observe the change both in the proportion of births to the deaths, and also to the marriages, which has taken place at Middleton (and I have received similar accounts of other places) during the course of the last century. The former may be explained by the greater encouragement to matrimony, from the increase of trade: The latter is of more difficult solution; though it is probable that the warmer cloathing, and better fare, which the poor now enjoy, may have contributed to it. Luxury, when carried to such a degree as to enervate the constitution, is unfavourable to population; but plenty of nutritive diet may well be regarded as a source of fruitfulness. The lower class of people, in this country, formerly lived upon the coarsest food. Wheat, an hundred years ago, was almost unknown to them; and so lately has it been cultivated in Lancashire, that it has scarcely yet acquired the name of

corn,

corn, which in general is applied only to barley, oats, and rye. Potatoes alfo are much improved by the prefent judicious method of growing and propagating them; and they now conftitute a moft wholefome and nourifhing part of our diet.

A physician, of the firft rank in his profeffion, has fuggefted to me, that tea may be confidered as a powerful aphrodifiac; and he imputes the amazing population of China, amongft other caufes, to the general ufe of it. But the Dutch, who drink large quantities of the infufion of this vegetable, are fo far from being remarkable for the number of their children, that I have been well informed, two births to a marriage is the common proportion in Holland (d).

It muft be acknowledged, however, that warm infufions of tea, by relaxing and augmenting the fenfibility of the fibres, which in cold climates, and in hard labouring people, are ufually too rigid and torpid, may promote the increafe of the human fpecies. But the obfervation is true only under certain limitations; for the fame caufe, by debilitating the conftitution beyond the due

(d) In China, the women are fo prolific, and the human fpecies multiplies fo faft, that the lands, though ever fo much cultivated, are fcarcely fufficient to fupport the inhabitants. Montefquieu.

medium,

medium, may operate in a contrary manner. Perhaps the general ufe of pepper, and of other fpices, may increafe the fertility of mankind.

But I fhall fufpend my conjectures for the prefent. A variety of caufes may counteract the operation of thofe which I have enumerated; and a confiderable number of facts muft be adduced to afcertain, whether the proportion of births to marriages be generally increafed in countries advanced from poverty to wealth, by the intro-duction of trade, or the improvement of agri-culture. The inftance of Middleton, and of one or two places more which firft occurred, and fuggefted the preceding obfervations, is oppofed by others which have lately fallen under my notice. And I cannot clofe this fubject better, than by giving a view of all the facts, which I have collected on both fides of the queftion.

A Table *fhewing the* Proportion *of* Births *to* Marriages *in different Places, and at different* Periods *of* Time.

MIDDLETON.

Year.	Marriages.	Chriftenings.	Births to a Marriage
From 1663 to 1672,	121	388 =	$3\frac{1}{5}$ +.
1763 to 1772,	330	1570 =	$4\frac{3}{4}$.

WARRINGTON.

WARRINGTON.

Year.	Marriages.	Christenings.	Births to a Marriage.
From 1702 to 1722,	131	385 =	2.9.
1752 to 1772,	1549	5034 =	$3\frac{1}{4}$.

PENTRAETH PARISH, ANGLESEY*.

From 1740 to 1747,	32	100 =	$3\frac{1}{3}$.
1764 to 1771,	33	149 =	$4\frac{1}{2}$.

LLANDYFNAN PARISH, ANGLESEY*.

From 1750 to 1757,	28	111 =	3.9+.
1764 to 1771,	32	154 =	$4\frac{4}{5}$+.
1547 to 1554,	8	36 =	$4\frac{1}{2}$.
1620 to 1627,	20	44 =	$2\frac{1}{5}$.

LEVERPOOL.

From 1700 to 1710,	500	2127 =	$4\frac{1}{4}$.
1762 to 1771,	4812	10010 =	$2\frac{1}{12}$.

BOWDEN.

From 1653 to 1662,	136	573 =	$4\frac{1}{5}$+.
1763 to 1772,	369	1300 =	$3\frac{1}{2}$+.

MANCHESTER.

From 1763 to 1773,	4396	11052 =	$2\frac{1}{17}$.

* See Philosophical Transactions, vol. LXIII.

I HAVE

I HAVE lately received from the Rev. Mr. Archdeacon Blackburne, Rector of Richmond in Yorkſhire, the following account of his pariſh. From the year 1764 to 1773 incluſive, 452 males, and 376 females have been baptiſed; and 299 males, and 341 females have been buried. The marriages during this period have amounted to 200. In Richmond there are about ſix hundred houſes; but the Eaſter Book enumerates only 450 families; and Mr. Blackburne computes the number of inhabitants to be 2300. " We have no diſtempers," he ſays, " that can be " called endemial; and when fevers prevail in the " neighbourhood, few are affected by them in " this town. If any perſon brings an ague to " Richmond, he is generally freed from it in a " few days; though the village of Gilling, about " a mile and a half diſtant, which ſtands low, and " has a large pool of ſtagnant water adjoining to " it, is viſited with this complaint every ſpring " and autumn.

" THE air of Richmond ſeems to be peculiarly " unfavourable to conſumptive diſorders. Many " ſtrangers come hither, from different parts, in " the firſt ſtage of the *phthiſis pulmonalis*; but, " after thirty-five years experience, I may truly " ſay that not one has recovered; although the " utmoſt care and attention has been paid to " their reſpective caſes. The natives and con-
" ſtant

" ftant refidents however are not fubject to
" diftempers of the lungs, except when brought
" on by intemperance. But rheumatic com-
" plaints are very general, efpecially amongft
" the fenior part of the inhabitants. In fmall
" corporation towns, like Richmond, numbers
" are taken off by exceffive drinking; but the
" people here who live temperately, feldom die
" earlier than in their eightieth year."

HAPPENING to pafs through Sutton-Coldfield
in Warwickfhire, laft fummer, I was very much
ftruck with the beauty and apparent healthfulnefs
of its fituation; and was defirous of knowing the
duration of life which the inhabitants of it enjoy.
The rector of the parifh has, with great polite-
nefs and good nature, gratified my curiofity, as
far as he is able, by furnifhing me with an extract from the church regifter, and by referring
me to the thirty-fecond volume of the Gentleman's
Magazine, for the following authentic account
of the place, drawn up, I fuppofe, by himfelf.

" SUTTON-COLDFIELD is almoft full fouth of
" Litchfield, at the diftance of about eight
" meafured miles, by which it undoubtedly got
" its name of Sutton, a contraction of South
" town: A remarkably bleak and barren com-
" mon, which lies directly weft of it, juft out
" of the bounds of the parifh, might probably
" give it the additional denomination of Cold-

VOL. II.   E   " field;

" field; the air being, upon that heath, as keen
" and cold as in the Highlands of Scotland.
" The parish is nearly oval in its figure; the
" longest diameter seven miles, and the breadth
" four. The face of it is agreeably diversified
" with gently rising hills, and vallies of tolerably
" fruitful meadows. It is bounded on the north
" by Kenston, on the west by Barr, on the south
" by Curdworth and Aston near Birmingham,
" and on the east by Middleton: It contains
" four hamlets, viz. Mancy, Hill, Little Sutton,
" and Warmley. In the year 1630, there were
" 298 houses in the parish; in 1698 there were
" 310; in 1721 the number was increased to
" 360, which is nearly about the number at
" present. I compute the inhabitants at 1800.
" The register begins in the year 1603. The
" number of christenings for the first 20 years
" of the register was 645; the burials during the
" same period were 501. The number of
" christenings for the last 20 years (ending at
" Christmas 1761) was 747; the burials
" 694 (a)."

It is curious to observe the almost exact proportion which the christenings bear to the burials,
in two very distant periods of time. But the
like proportion seems to hold no longer. For

(a) Gentleman's Magazine for September 1762, p. 401.

from

from 1762 to 1772 the births have been 655, the deaths 445. The vicinity of Birmingham, and the amazing extenſion of its manufactures, will account for this change; which ſeems to have ariſen from the recruits annually drawn from Sutton-Coldfield, as well as from every other adjacent place. If the number of inhabit- ants in this town be rightly computed, the yearly mortality amongſt them is only as 1 to 51; and every houſe, at a medium, contains five perſons.

IT appears by the obſervations lately com- municated to me by the Rev. Doctor Tucker, that the number of females baptized at the pariſh church of St. Stephen's in Briſtol, from 1754 to 1774, has exceeded the number of males bap- tized during the ſame period of time; and that the like remark has been made in ſome other pariſhes of the ſame city. From theſe facts the learned Dean concludes, that Dr. Derham's cal- culation, which ſuppoſes the proportion of male to female births to be as 14 to 13, may proba- bly be erroneous; and he expreſſes his earneſt wiſh, that further inquiry may be made into a ſubject of ſo much importance. The following table will ſhew the reſult of the few obſervations which I have collected.

A COMPARATIVE VIEW *of the* NUMBER *of* MALES
and FEMALES, BAPTIZED *in different Places.*

Places.	Males.	Females.
Difhley, 11 years -	149	145
St. Stephen's Parifh, Briftol,		
20 years - -	591	607
Taxal, 16 years - -	204	230
Richmond, 10 years -	452	376
Middleton, 10 years -	200	188
Bowden, 10 years -	663	639
Middlewich, 5 years -	229	242
Chapel in le Frith, 10 years	451	332
Warrington, 1 year -	175	181
Collegiate Church in Man-		
chefter, 7 years -	3215	3024
Royton, 10 years -	134	120
Chefter, 2 years -	408	415
Total	6871	6499

FROM this table it appears, that the proportion of males to females baptized is nearly as
12 to 11; but the fucceeding ones fhew, that
the number of females alive confiderably exceeds
the number of males, in a variety of places;
and that the widows are almoft double the
number of widowers.

A COMPARATIVE

A COMPARATIVE VIEW *of the* NUMBER *of* MALES *and* FEMALES *in different Places.*

Places.	Males.	Females.
Manchefter -	10548	11933
Salford - -	2248	2517
Townfhips of ditto	947	958
Parifh of Manchefter	6942	6844
Bolton - -	2159	2392
Little Bolton -	361	410
Monton - -	196	190
Hale - -	140	136
Horwich - -	149	156
Darwen - -	900	950
Cockey - -	320	391
Chowbent - -	554	606
Ackworth - -	340	388
Eaftham - -	451	461
Chinley - -	181	168
Brownfide -	40	47
Bugfworth -	80	95
Afhton under line	1406	1453
Parifh of ditto	2584	2513
Tattenhall Parifh	382	399
Waverton Parifh	310	332
Total	31238	33339

E 3 A COMPARATIVE

A COMPARATIVE VIEW *of the* NUMBER *of* WIDOWERS *and* WIDOWS, *in different Places.*

Places.	Widowers.	Widows.
Manchefter - -	432	1064
Salford - - -	89	149
Townfhip of ditto -	21	42
Parifh of Manchefter -	232	315
Monton - - -	14	13
Hale - - -	8	12
Horwich - - -	9	8
Darwen - - -	30	48
Cockey - - -	10	27
Chowbent - -	26	43
Chinley, Brownfide, and		
Bugfworth - -	15	18
Afhton under line -	50	81
Parifh of ditto - -	67	95
Total	1003	1915

LET no arguments in favour of polygamy be drawn from thefe tables! The practice is brutal; deftructive to friendfhip and moral fentiment; inconfiftent with one great end of marriage, the education of children; and fub-verfive of the natural rights of more than half of the fpecies.

- - - Higher

- - - - - Higher of the genial bed by far,
And with myfterious reverence I deem.
MILTON.

Nor is this tyranny of man over the weaker, but more amiable fex, favourable to population. For notwithftanding the number of females in the world may confiderably exceed the number of males, yet there are more men capable of propagating their fpecies, than women capable of bearing children. This painful office gradually becomes more dangerous, and lefs frequent, as the rigidnefs of the fibres increafes; and ceafes entirely at the age of fifty. The fatality of it is thus wifely obviated, and the comforts of declining life are not interrupted by the arduous toil of nurfing. An inftitution therefore which confines in fervile bondage to one ufurper, many females in the prime of youth, muft leave numbers deftitute of the means which nature has pointed out, for perpetuating and increafing the race of mankind. And it is a fact well known, that Armenia, in which a plurality of wives is not allowed, abounds more with inhabitants than any other province of the Turkifh Empire.

JUNE 5, 1774.

E 4   P. S. SINCE

———————

P. S. SINCE the preceding paper was written, the Rev. Mr. Craddock has favoured me with a furvey of the town and parifh of Afhton under line, diftant about eight miles from Manchefter; and, alfo, with an account of the burials and chriftenings, during the laft eleven years. The inhabitants of this place confift of manufacturers and farmers.

An ENUMERATION *of the* INHABITANTS *of the* Town *and* Parifh *of* ASHTON UNDER LINE, *made in* 1775.

	Town.	Parifh.
Inhabitants -	2859	5097
Houfes - -	553	941
Families - -	599	971
Males - -	1406	2584
Females - -	1453	2513
Married - -	982	1679
Widowers - -	50	67
Widows - -	81	95
Under five years of age	509	896
From five to ten	396	764
ten to twenty	541	1011
twenty to fifty	1044	1882
fifty to feventy	307	471
feventy to ninety	62	73

An

An Account of the BURIALS *and* CHRISTENINGS *in the Parish of* ASHTON UNDER LINE, *during the last eleven Years.*

BURIALS.

	Males unmarried.	Females Do.	Husbands.	Wives.	Widowers.	Widows.	
1765	159	60	51	10	17	13	8
1766	187	42	54	34	24	7	26
1767	159	44	45	23	21	9	17
1768	197	69	60	18	25	1	24
1769	206	79	75	16	12	9	15
1770	167	54	46	29	7	20	11
1771	178	67	43	26	23	8	11
1772	250	97	71	16	35	10	21
1773	157	48	50	18	23	6	12
1774	152	38	46	21	24	10	13
1775	241	92	96	15	20	8	10
	2053	690	637	226	231	101	168

CHRISTENINGS.

	Males.	Females.
1765	121	114
1766	97	123
1767	116	111
1768	122	108
1769	157	137

1770

	Males.	Females.
1770	139	142
1771	133	143
1772	168	141
1773	174	131
1774	137	146
1775	168	164
	1532	1460

THE Reverend Dr. Peploe, Chancellor of the diocefe of Chefter, has honoured me with the following account of the parifhes of Waverton and Tattenhall, both in the neighbourhood of Chefter. The inhabitants are farmers and labourers.

An ENUMERATION *of the* INHABITANTS *of* TATTENHALL, *made in Auguft* 1774, *by the Reverend* BRICE STORR, *Curate*.

Inhabited houfes - - -	148.
Uninhabited ditto - - -	2.
Heads of families - - -	176.
Aged above fifteen years - -	462.
Men and boys - - -	382.
Women and girls - - -	399.

CHRISTENINGS.

	CHRISTENINGS.	BURIALS.
1764	28	8
1765	21	9
1766	19	12
1767	29	11
1768	28	16
1769	24	15
1770	37	15
1771	30	9
1772	26	15
1773	38	20
	280	130

An ENUMERATION *of the* INHABITANTS *of* WA-VERTON, *made in August* 1774, *by the Reverend* Mr. BISSELL, *Minister of the Parish.*

Inhabited houses	109
Uninhabited ditto	2
Heads of families	116
Aged above fourteen years	406
Men and boys	310
Women and girls	332

	CHRISTENINGS.	BURIALS.
1764	19	10
1765	26	2
1766	17	7
1767	18	10

	CHRISTENINGS.	BURIALS.
1768	22	10
1769	17	7
1770	20	8
1771	23	9
1772	18	12
1773	13	9
	193	84

EXTRACT *of a* LETTER *from the Reverend Mr.* BISSELL, *of* WAVERTON *near* CHESTER.

At the beginning of the year 1775, the parish of Waverton near Chester, contained

Inhabited Houses.	Families.	Males.	Females.	Inhabitants.
111.	116.	310.	332.	642.

From Jan. 1ft to Dec. 31ft 1775 inclusive there were

CHRISTENINGS.		BURIALS.	
Males	14	Males	6
Females	8	Females	6
	22		12

BURIALS IN 1775.

Days.	Sex.	Age.	Diseases.
Jan. 20,	A Woman	77 Years	Asthma.
Jan. 31,	A Girl	9 Weeks	Convulsions.
Feb. 9,	A Woman	67 Years	Dropsy.
March 6,	A Woman	87 Years	Decay of Age, and an Ulcer in the Axilla.

April

Days.	Sex.	Age.	Difeafes.
April 3,	A Woman	65 Years	Putrid Fever.
April 9,	A Man	45 Years	Uncertain.
April 11,	A Man	63 Years	Dropfy.
June 18,	A Woman	40 Years	Confumption.
July 6,	A Boy	14 Months	Small Pox with hot Regimen.
Aug. 14,	A Boy	4 Years	Small Pox and Worms.
Nov. 11,	A Man	65 Years	Gout and Dropfy in confequence of hard drinking.
Nov. 26,	A Man	68 Years	Dropfy.

In the valuable work which I have fo often quoted, Dr. Price has advanced many arguments to fhew the declining ftate of population in this kingdom. The growth of large towns, the prevalence of vice and luxury, the difcouragements to marriage, the deftruction of cottages, and various other caufes, have the moft unfavourable influence on the increafe of mankind. But it is to be hoped, that thefe evils do not generally prevail, and that even fome good may arife from them to check their baneful effects. Certain it is, that in this part of England the inhabitants multiply with great rapidity: And though the increafe may be chiefly owing to recruits drawn from other counties, yet the flourifhing ftate of our manufactures cannot fail to promote population, by affording plentiful

means

means of fubfiftence to the poor. The Bifhop
of Chefter (Dr. Markham) informs me, that in
various parifh regifters which he has confulted,
the births have progreffively become more
numerous from generation to generation. At
Broxley in Kent, where his Lordfhip was Vicar,
he divided the times, from the commencement of
the reign of Queen Elizabeth, into periods of
twenty-one years; and found, that the number of
births in the firft period was 310, and in the laft
525. The increafe was gradual through the
whole time.

APPENDIX

TO THE FOREGOING OBSERVATIONS.

THE following view of the progrefs of population, in Manchefter, from 1758 to 1777, inclufive, divided into periods of five years,
was annexed to the yearly bill of mortality,
A. D. 1778.

	Average Number of Deaths including Diffenters.	Number of Inhabitants eftimated by fuppofing the Deaths to be 1 in 28,4.	Progreffive Increafe.
From 1758 to 1762	751	21,328	——.
1763 to 1767	869	24,680	3,352.
1768 to 1772	958	27,246	2,566.
1773 to 1777	1010	28,684	1,438.

DURING

During the laft-mentioned period, viz. from 1773 to 1777, 719 houfes were built in Manchefter and Salford. At the clofe of 1777, 151 of thefe were uninhabited.

By a furvey, completed in December, 1783, of the townfhips of Manchefter and Salford, the number of houfes was found be 6195; which number multiplied, as formerly, by $6\frac{1}{3}$ would make the inhabitants to have then amounted to 39,235. But it is probable, that the proportion of $6\frac{1}{3}$ to a houfe, is lefs than the truth, at a period when the reftoration of peace produced a fudden influx of people. And the increafe of population has been fince fo great, that the enumeration at Chriftmas, 1788, ftood as follows:

	Houfes.	Families.	Perfons.
Townfhip of Manchefter,	5916	8570	42821.
Townfhip of Salford, about,	1260	——	——

In Salford, the houfes being generally fmaller than in Manchefter, Mr. Wharmby, the furveyor to whom I am indebted for this account, is of opinion, that fix perfons may be reckoned to each dwelling. The whole number of inhabitants, therefore, in the two townfhips, exceeds 50,000.

The rapid growth of Manchefter admits of an eafy and fatisfactory explanation, from the aftonifhing and fudden increafe of the cotton manufactory, of which it may be deemed the

great

great *emporium*. Not more than twenty years fince, it is faid, the whole annual return of this trade in Great Britain amounted only to £200,000 : Whereas, at this time, the grofs produce of raw materials and labour is eftimated at more than feven millions fterling. And it is calculated, that one hundred and fifty-nine thoufand men, ninety thoufand women, and a hundred and one thoufand children are employed in the different ftages of the manufacture *(b)*.

I HAVE mentioned an obfervation, communicated by Dr. Tucker, that the number of females baptized at the parifh church of St. Stephen's, in Briftol, from 1754 to 1774, exceeded the number of males baptized during the fame period of time; and that, from hence, the learned Dean fufpected Dr. Derham's calculation to be erroneous, which makes the proportion of male to female births to be as 14 to 13. From the facts which I collected, the proportion appeared to be nearly as 12 to 11 : But Dr. Price, from a much larger induction, has now fully fhewn, that it is as 20 to 19 *(c)*.

(b) See a Pamphlet entitled, an Important Crifis in the Callico and Muflin Manufactory. 1788.

(c) Reverfionary Payments, vol. II. fourth edit. p. 16. Appendix.

IT

It has been evinced, by a great variety of regifters, that the mortality of males exceeds that of females, in almoft every period of life; but efpecially in the earlieft ftages of it, nearly one half more of the former than of the latter being ftill born; and, that the excefs prevails moft in great towns, and under other circum-ftances, which are unfavourable to health. Dr. Clarke, phyfician to the Lying-in Hofpital at Dublin, has elucidated this intricate fubjeft, in a paper read before the Royal Society, March 30, 1786. Male fœtufes, being larger, require more nutrition than female fœtufes, during geftation; and are more liable to injury at the time of birth. Debility, therefore, in either parent, from whatever fource it may arife, muft affeft that fex the moft, both before and after delivery, which not only requires the largeft and ftrongeft *ftamina*, but is put to the fevereft trials, both in delivery and in after-life.

Among the caufes which increafe the pro-portion of human mortality, in large towns, muft be reckoned the more ready communica-tion and greater malignity of contagious dif-tempers. In June 1783, I received the follow-ing information from Richard Townley, Efq. of Belfield, near Rochdale, a very refpeftable and intelligent juftice of the peace. I fhall de-

liver it in his own words. " It is unneceffary
" to make any apology for fending you an
" account of the ravages, which that dreadful
" diforder, the fmall-pox, made in the town
" of Rochdale, within the fpace of a few months,
" laft winter, compared with the ftate of thofe
" children, who happened to be infected with
" the fame loathfome malady, in two villages
" nearly adjoining to my houfe, during the
" fame period of time. The account is very
" accurate, being taken by the conftables,
" who went from houfe to houfe ; and it
" is found to agree with the parifh regifter.
" The latter table is delivered from my own
" perfonal knowledge."

	No. Ill.	Dead.	Recovered.
Part of Huddersfield town-fhip, within Rochdale,	141	40	101
Spotland townfhip, -	108	30	78
Caftleton ditto, -	160	32	128
	409	102	307
In the village of Belfield,	20	0	20
Ditto Newbold,	19	1	18
	39	1	38

Dr. Smith, in the Wealth of Nations, obferves, that it is not uncommon, in the Highlands

lands of Scotland, for a woman to have only two furviving children of twenty whom fhe has brought into the world. But a life of rural labour, in a tolerably genial climate, without extreme penury, is favourable to population. At Dunmow in Effex, we are informed, the parifh contains 262 poor families, who have 460 children. There are alfo 116 families of the ranks above them, who have only 120 children, which is little more than half the former proportion. The *ratio* of deaths, during the laft five years, has been, of the poor children 1 in 45½; of thofe in a higher ftation 1 in 37½ *(d)*.

(d) See Howlett on the Increafe of the Poor. 1783. p. 102.

OBSERVATIONS

ON THE

INCREASE AND DECREASE

OF

DIFFERENT DISEASES,

AND PARTICULARLY OF THE PLAGUE.

By WILLIAM HEBERDEN, Jun. M.D. F.R.S.

LONDON:

Printed for T. PAYNE, at the Mews-Gate.

1801.

Republished in 1973 by Gregg International Publishers Limited
Westmead, Farnborough, Hants., England

ADVERTISEMENT.

THE following Remarks were put together with the intention of subjoining them to a new edition of the Bills of Mortality. In submitting them separately to the Public, the Author is influenced by no vanity, or self-conceit, no forwardness to broach new opinions, nor any wish to support a favourite system. If he has stated any thing as fact, he has at least endeavoured to do it fairly; or if he has hazarded any conclusions, he has at the same time laid open the sources from which they were drawn. His object is to direct the attention of the Medical world to a subject which has hitherto been very much neglected; and which appears to him capable of being employed to valuable purposes.

PREFACE.

PEOPLE have fallen into two oppofite errors concerning the Bills of Mortality. Some have confidered their authority as too vague to be made the foundation of any certain conclufions; and others have built upon this foundation, without fufficiently confidering it's real defects. Both parties are equally in the wrong.

THE agreement of the Bills with each other, does alone carry with it a ftrong proof, that the numbers under the feveral articles are by no means fet down at random; but muft be taken from the uniform operation of fome permanent caufe. While the gradual changes they exhibit in particular difeafes, correfpond to the alterations which in time are known to take place in the channels through which the great ftream of mortality is conftantly flowing.

THAT there are, however, many and very great imperfections in the Bills of Mortality, cannot be doubted. For, firft, the births include only thofe who are baptized according to the rites and ufage of the Church of England. By which

means

means all Jews, Quakers, Papifts, and the very numerous body of Diffenters, are omitted. And though fome among the poorer fort both of Papifts, and Diffenters, who live at a diftance from their refpective burial-grounds, and cannot bear the expence of being carried thither, are buried according to the rites of the Eftablifhed Church, and confequently have a place in the regifter ; yet the numbers fo accounted for, muft be very few compared with the deficiencies.

SECONDLY : Of thofe who are of the Church of England, a very large proportion are either buried in the country, or in burial grounds adjacent to London, but without the Bills. The burials alfo in St. Paul's Cathedral, in Weftminfter Abbey, the Temple, the Rolls, Lincoln's Inn, St. Peter's in the Tower, the Charterhoufe, the feveral Hofpitals of the metropolis, and other places which are not parochial cemeteries, are for that reafon omitted. Befides which, the great parifhes of Marybone, and Pancras, have never yet had a place in the Bills of Mortality. In the former of thefe alone, the burials, on an average of five years, from 1795 to 1799 inclufive, amounted annually to 1,550 (a).

THIRDLY : Many abortives and ftill-born, making together above 700 in the year, are noticed in the deaths, but not in the births.

FOURTHLY,

(a) Mr. Pennant, in his Account of London, fays, it is the opinion of Mr. Richardfon, who has ferved the parifh offices, that there are nearly as many buried from London, at different burial grounds, without, as within the limits of the Bills of Mortality.

FOURTHLY: The miſtakes and miſrepreſentations, to which the particular diſeaſes are liable, are too obvious to be inſiſted upon. Yet it deſerves to be repeated, that even in theſe ſmaller diviſions of the ſubject, the correſpondence of one year, and of one week, with another, is ſuch, as muſt convince every attentive obſerver, that a conſiderable degree of credit is due to their report.

ERRATUM:

Page 95. Note *(p)* *for* page 66, *read* page 31.

TABLE I.

OF the ANNUAL CHRISTENINGS and BURIALS in LONDON for each Year of the Eighteenth Century; Together with the Proportion out of every Thouſand, who have died by Bowel Complaints, Small Pox, Palſy, Meaſles, or Childbirth.—*From the Bills of Mortality.*

TABLE I.

Years - -	1701	1702	1703	1704	1705	1706	1707	1708	1709	1710	Average
CHRISTENED	15616	15687	15448	15895	16145	15369	16066	15862	15220	14928	15623
BURIED - -	20471	19481	20720	22684	22097	19847	21600	21291	21800	24620	21461
Flux - - ⎫ Colic - - ⎬ Gripes - - ⎭	60.8	67	53	56	52.6	50.4	45.9	41.1	42.4	32.9	50.2
Small Pox -	53.1	15.9	43.3	66.1	49.7	36	49.9	79.2	46.6	126.7	56.6
Apoplexy - ⎫ Palfy - - ⎬ Suddenly - ⎭	8	6.9	7.6	6.4	7.1	7.8	7.2	8	7.4	6.6	7.3
Meafles - -	0.2	1.4	2.4	0.5	14.5	18	1.7	5.9	4	7.3	5.5
Childbed - ⎫ Mifcarriage ⎭	10 9	11.4	10.5	11.7	13	11.9	11.9	11.5	9.8	8.8	11.1

Years - -	1711	1712	1713	1714	1715	1716	1717	1718	1719	1720	Average
CHRISTENED	14706	15660	15927	17495	17234	17421	18475	18307	18413	17479	17111
BURIED - -	19833	21198	21057	26569	22232	24436	23446	26523	28347	25454	23909
Flux - - ⎫ Colic - - ⎬ Gripes - - ⎭	35.7	32.5	33.8	30.2	32.3	33.9	35.8	39.1	39.5	38.3	35.2
Small Pox -	45.7	92.5	76.8	106	48	99.4	94.4	71	114.1	56.7	80.4
Apoplexy - ⎫ Palfy - - ⎬ Suddenly - ⎭	9	7.4	9.3	7.5	8.4	7.5	10.3	8.5	8.5	9.9	8.6
Meafles - -	4.8	3.6	2.9	5.2	1.3	11	1.5	18.5	8.5	8.3	6.5
Childbed - ⎫ Mifcarriage ⎭	9.8	9.8	8.4	11.6	12.5	9.4	10.3	9.9	10.3	10.2	10.2

TABLE I.—*continued.*

Years - -	1721	1722	1723	1724	1725	1726	1727	1728	1729	1730	Average
CHRISTENED	18370	18339	19203	19370	18859	18808	18252	16652	17060	17118	18203
BURIED - -	26142	25750	29197	25952	25523	29647	28418	27810	29722	26761	27492
Flux - -⎫ Colic - - ⎬ Gripes - -⎭	32.6	32.2	36.3	34.1	26.4	25.4	24.3	20.2	19.3	18.5	26.9
Small Pox -	91.3	84.3	112.8	47.2	125	53	83.7	75.2	95.9	71.6	84
Apoplexy -⎫ Palfy - - ⎬ Suddenly -⎭	9.6	8.6	8.2	9.6	8.7	8	8	7.2	7.4	10	8.5
Meafles - -	9.1	4.4	7.9	4.5	2.7	8.6	2.5	3	1.3	11.6	5.6
Childbed -⎫ Mifcarriage ⎬	11.5	11.4	10	9.5	10.4	8.3	7.9	7.7	8.4	10	9.5

Years - -	1731	1732	1733	1734	1735	1736	1737	1738	1739	1740	Average
CHRISTENED	17830	17788	17465	17630	16873	16491	16760	16060	16181	15231	16830
BURIED - -	25262	23358	29233	26062	23538	27581	27823	25825	25432	30811	26492
Flux - -⎫ Colic - - ⎬ Gripes - -⎭	15.7	15.9	12.2	14.9	14.7	14.3	13	11.9	11.7	10.3	13.4
Small Pox -	105.6	51.3	47.2	103.4	67.8	109.6	74.4	61.1	66.5	85.2	77.1
Apoplexy -⎫ Palfy - - ⎬ Suddenly -⎭	11	11.4	9.0	8.4	10	9.1	9.9	8.9	9	8.8	9.5
Meafles - -	4.1	1.3	20.8	0.7	0.4	6.1	4.5	8.3	12.8	1.4	7.0
Childbed -⎫ Mifcarriage ⎬	10.3	9 5	10.3	10.5	8.3	7.4	10.1	10	10.3	7.5	9.4

TABLE I.—*continued.*

Years	1741	1742	1743	1744	1745	1746	1747	1748	1749	1750	Average
CHRISTENED	14957	13751	15050	14261	14078	14577	14942	14153	14260	14545	14458
BURIED	32169	27483	25200	20606	21296	28157	25494	23869	25516	23727	25352
Flux / Colic / Gripes	9.6	5.7	6.6	4.7	8.7	6.4	7.6	7	7.5	7.4	7.1
Small Pox	61.7	52.1	81.1	79.2	57.4	115.5	54.3	74.6	102.9	51.8	72
Apoplexy / Palsy / Suddenly	8.6	10.5	11	12.4	12	11.2	9.6	12.6	12.7	14	11.4
Measles	1.3	35.8	0.7	0.2	0.6	8.9	3.1	0.4	4.1	13.5	6.8
Childbed / Miscarriage	8.1	7.5	7.1	9	9.4	6.8	8.3	8.5	7.3	9.7	8.1

Years	1751	1752	1753	1754	1755	1756	1757	1758	1759	1760	Average
CHRISTENED	14691	15308	15444	14947	15209	14830	14053	14209	14253	14951	14789
BURIED	21028	20485	19276	22696	21917	20872	21313	17576	19604	19830	20460
Flux / Colic / Gripes	6.6	6.6	7.3	6	4.3	4	3.5	3.5	4.3	2.7	4.8
Small Pox	47.5	173.4	40.7	104.3	90.4	77.3	154.7	72.7	132.4	104.5	102.7
Apoplexy / Palsy / Suddenly	13.5	12.6	15.6	13.6	12	15	12.2	14.7	11.7	14.4	13.5
Measles	1	5.4	13.3	0.5	19.2	7.5	1.1	39.7	16.6	8.8	11.5
Childbed / Miscarriage	8.4	7.9	9.1	9.6	9.5	8.6	8.4	10.6	10.3	12	9.4

TABLE I.—*continued.*

Years - -	1761	1762	1763	1764	1765	1766	1767	1768	1769	1770	Average
CHRISTENED	16000	15351	15133	16801	16374	16257	15980	16042	16714	17109	16176
BURIED - -	21063	26326	26143	23202	23230	23911	22612	23639	21847	22434	23441
Flux - -⎫ Colic - -⎬ Gripes - -⎭	4	7.9	3.4	3.4	2.8	2.8	3.2	4.1	3	3.5	3.8
Small Pox -	72.6	105.2	137.7	103.4	108.6	97.2	96.8	128.3	89.4	88.5	102.7
Apoplexy -⎫ Palsy - -⎬ Suddenly -⎭	15.7	13.6	11.4	12.6	11.4	12.9	14	9.7	12	13	12.6
Measles - -	19	4.6	23.4	2.8	2.3	20	3.5	17.3	4	14.5	11.1
Childed -⎫ Miscarriage⎭	14	10.6	9.9	10.2	10.8	8.5	7.8	9	8.6	12.2	11.1

Years - -	1771	1772	1773	1774	1775	1776	1777	1778	1779	1780	Average
CHRISTENED	17072	17916	16805	16998	17629	17280	18300	17300	16769	16634	17170
BURIED - -	21780	26053	21656	20884	20514	19048	23334	20399	20420	20517	21460
Flux - -⎫ Colic - -⎬ Gripes - -⎭	2.5	2.7	2.7	3.8	4	2.9	2.1	2.9	4.2	4.5	3.2
Small Pox -	76.5	153.5	48.1	119.1	130.2	90.9	110.1	70.2	122.2	42.5	96.3
Apoplexy -⎫ Palsy - -⎬ Suddenly -⎭	13.4	12.4	13.1	13.5	13.6	16.8	14.1	14.8	12.6	16.8	14.1
Measles - -	5.3	8.1	9.2	5.8	13.8	8	6.2	19.1	4.8	13.2	9,3
Childbed -⎫ Miscarriage⎭	8.2	7.5	9	9,9	9.3	10.2	9.6	8.6	10.4	9.3	9.2

TABLE I.—*continued.*

Years - -	1781	1782	1783	1784	1785	1786	1787	1788	1789	1790	Average
CHRISTENED	17026	17101	17091	17179	17919	18119	17508	19559	18163	1898	17862
BURIED - -	20709	17918	19029	17828	18919	20454	19349	19697	20749	18038	19269
Flux - Colic - Gripes -	4.5	2.4	3.4	1	1.6	1.5	0.7	1.5	1.3	0.6	1.8
Small Pox -	169.5	35.5	81.6	97.7	105.3	60.5	126	55.8	101.1	89.8	92.2
Apoplexy - Palfy - Suddenly -	13.4	19.5	15.4	15.2	16.5	15	12.8	14.8	14.4	15.5	15.2
Meafles - -	9.7	9.4	9.7	1.6	1	39.5	4.6	2.8	26	6.6	11
Childbed - Mifcarriage	10.1	7.7	7.6	7.6	8.8	10	11.3	10	8.5	8.3	9

Years - -	1791	1792	1793	1794	1795	1796	1797	1798	1799	1800	Average
CHRISTENED	18496	19348	19108	18689	18361	18826	18645	17927	18970	19176	18754
BURIED - -	18760	20213	21749	19241	21179	19288	17014	18155	18134	23068	19680
Flux - Colic - Gripes -	0.8	0.5	1.1	0.9	0.9	1.1	0.9	1.4	0.7	1	0.9
Small Pox -	94.5	78.4	109.7	100.7	49.5	183.9	30.7	128.7	61.3	104.7	94.2
Apoplexy - Palfy - Suddenly -	15	15	16.2	14.7	14.2	15.4	18.4	17.1	19.5	16.3	16.2
Meafles - -	6.6	22.5	11.4	9	15.6	15.9	13	10.8	12.3	17.2	13.4
Childbed - Mifcarriage	8.5	10	8.7	9.5	7	10.5	12.2	8	7.4	7.3	8.9

T A B L E II.

OF Ten different Articles extracted from the LONDON WEEKLY BILLS OF MORTALITY, fhewing their Variations every Week for Ten Years.

TABLE II.

Weekly Bills of Mortality. 1763.	Whole Number buried.	Under two years.	Above fixty years.	Apoplexy, Palfy, Suddenly.	Childbed and Mifcarriage.	Confumptions.	Fever.	Colic, Flux, Gripes, Loofenefs.	Meafles.	Small Pox.
4 Jan. - -	641	197	93	11	2	113	73	9	0	106
11 Jan. - -	565	162	84	6	3	104	55	5	0	108
18 Jan. - -	583	146	86	11	8	118	61	1	0	107
25 Jan. - -	621	149	105	5	13	103	62	3	2	113
1 Feb. - -	687	216	128	14	10	129	59	2	3	125
8 Feb. - -	612	152	120	5	8	106	76	4	1	84
15 Feb. - -	520	146	86	4	6	93	43	2	3	95
22 Feb. - -	551	158	86	6	5	108	69	3	1	79
1 Mar. - -	469	126	65	6	5	108	54	1	2	67
8 Mar. - -	513	153	86	3	7	103	64	0	0	65
15 Mar. - -	404	98	76	3	0	93	29	1	2	51
22 Mar. - -	552	157	87	3	3	114	75	2	1	73
29 Mar. - -	443	135	59	4	3	106	53	3	2	52
5 Apr. - -	448	131	79	6	6	85	62	1	2	57
12 Apr. - -	484	147	78	5	4	108	63	0	3	57
19 Apr. - -	477	141	68	6	7	83	49	0	8	61
26 Apr. - -	505	140	76	5	6	105	83	0	7	54
3 May - -	461	135	70	3	9	101	36	0	7	61
10 May - -	567	159	85	9	12	105	68	0	12	77
17 May - -	484	155	60	6	3	81	70	0	15	52
24 May - -	452	152	70	5	2	88	54	2	14	49
31 May - -	537	179	72	7	10	118	43	1	15	67
7 June - -	524	174	70	7	7	87	69	1	23	64
14 June - -	537	167	75	6	2	90	64	0	31	62
21 June - -	466	142	53	6	3	83	72	0	36	57
28 June - -	552	159	74	2	4	104	71	1	34	83

TABLE II.—*continued.*

WEEKLY BILLS of MORTALITY. 1763.	Whole Number buried.	Under two Years.	Above sixty Years.	Apoplexy, Palfy, Suddenly.	Childbed and Mifcarriage.	Confumption.	Fever.	Colic, Flux, Gripes, Loofenefs.	Meafles.	Small Pox.
5 July - -	533	161	60	5	11	96	82	0	34	69
12 July - -	517	163	64	11	7	76	60	1	36	80
19 July - -	506	175	56	4	2	90	66	3	51	78
26 July - -	486	192	46	3	5	78	62	3	20	87
2 Aug. - -	436	157	43	6	2	62	55	1	33	86
9 Aug. - -	460	192	47	5	2	65	62	3	26	69
16 Aug. - -	462	160	46	6	7	74	63	3	27	73
23 Aug. - -	548	146	72	1	4	105	75	1	15	66
30 Aug. - -	418	163	24	3	2	65	57	2	21	47
6 Sept. - -	478	174	69	5	1	74	67	2	16	59
13 Sept. - -	477	162	49	2	4	80	73	2	18	46
20 Sept. - -	516	185	60	6	4	90	73	6	14	51
27 Sept. - -	565	212	55	3	6	105	84	2	20	69
4 Oct. - -	485	174	68	6	4	83	64	5	13	50
11 Oct. - -	404	138	55	3	0	77	55	1	7	46
18 Oct. - -	473	153	69	6	2	97	77	4	4	47
25 Oct. - -	498	168	80	15	2	81	75	1	5	65
1 Nov. - -	384	122	55	3	6	79	55	2	4	45
8 Nov. - -	478	136	67	9	4	92	75	2	4	56
15 Nov. - -	362	112	49	3	6	72	67	2	7	46
22 Nov. - -	498	167	70	8	4	91	77	1	6	62
29 Nov. - -	511	172	78	8	4	91	77	1	6	57
6 Dec. - -	564	169	87	3	2	126	90	2	5	54
13 Dec. - -	480	163	58	9	4	110	85	1	1	38
20 Dec. - -	484	160	66	6	2	93	83	0	3	53
27 Dec. - -	380	125	41	2	5	77	59	1	4	37

C

TABLE II.—continued.

WEEKLY BILLS of MORTALITY. 1764.	Whole Number buried.	Under two Years.	Above fixty Years.	Apoplexy, Palfy, Suddenly.	Childbed and Mifcarriage.	Confumption.	Fever.	Colic, Flux, Gripes, Loofenefs.	Meafles.	Small Pox.
3 Jan. - -	585	207	76	8	7	116	84	4	4	44
10 Jan. - -	462	153	71	6	8	89	63	2	3	44
17 Jan. - -	499	176	69	7	4	97	78	2	0	37
24 Jan. - -	505	160	90	7	7	105	81	2	2	41
31 Jan. - -	466	142	62	4	7	95	86	2	1	26
7 Feb. - -	483	149	68	4	4	110	63	1	2	31
14 Feb. - -	504	162	84	5	8	103	79	3	4	28
21 Feb. - -	491	159	86	5	6	99	82	2	0	33
28 Feb. - -	447	130	70	10	6	86	70	3	2	27
6 Mar. - -	466	131	84	6	3	102	74	1	2	37
13 Mar. - -	519	158	99	3	2	94	80	1	1	41
20 Mar. - -	481	137	90	5	4	91	88	3	1	27
27 Mar. - -	463	147	83	6	4	99	72	2	1	29
3 Apr. - -	455	131	82	4	4	103	84	0	2	24
10 Apr. - -	402	109	59	6	1	93	76	0	2	22
17 Apr. - -	433	143	57	9	10	100	63	0	1	29
24 Apr. - -	405	129	60	3	2	89	62	1	0	33
1 May - -	405	131	57	11	4	76	62	3	0	37
8 May - -	435	130	61	7	4	92	56	0	0	47
15 May - -	420	129	67	7	5	87	69	0	4	30
22 May - -	381	126	51	3	1	76	52	1	0	32
29 May - -	409	120	51	3	2	80	69	5	2	39
5 June - -	421	138	47	1	5	93	58	3	1	39
12 June - -	415	132	71	6	5	83	72	1	2	44
19 June - -	407	135	49	6	6	79	62	5	1	55
26 June - -	398	126	52	4	3	60	70	2	1	44

TABLE II.—*continued.*

WEEKLY BILLS of MORTALITY. 1764.	Whole Number buried.	Under two Years.	Above fixty Years.	Apoplexy, Palfy, Suddenly.	Childbed and Mifcarriage.	Confumption.	Fever.	Colic, Flux, Gripes, Loofenefs	Meafles.	Small Pox.
July - -	402	119	51	2	2	76	70	2	2	55
10 July -	409	124	45	3	7	82	60	2	2	63
17 July - -	367	135	50	6	3	68	61	0	0	42
24 July - -	404	172	40	5	6	77	68	2	0	54
31 July - -	328	136	52	6	8	63	57	2	1	56
7 Aug. - -	395	153	41	7	3	68	60	3	0	48
14 Aug. - -	338	122	49	1	2	45	69	1	2	42
21 Aug. - -	388	151	48	7	3	55	73	1	0	44
28 Aug. - -	475	180	40	4	3	78	95	0	0	62
4 Sept. - -	457	189	49	7	5	65	86	2	0	56
11 Sept. - -	484	190	65	4	5	76	82	2	1	52
18 Sept. - -	486	215	56	7	1	86	80	3	2	63
25 Sept. - -	468	191	59	2	5	80	86	4	1	36
2 Oct. - -	477	171	67	5	4	85	88	2	0	52
9 Oct. - -	390	154	53	1	1	63	63	2	0	50
16 Oct. - -	466	163	50	2	6	83	81	3	2	57
23 Oct. - -	451	156	51	6	2	87	89	1	0	64
30 Oct. - -	440	135	57	5	4	89	63	2	2	69
6 Nov. - -	405	127	50	6	5	84	66	1	2	58
13 Nov. - -	538	153	80	14	10	88	106	0	1	88
20 Nov. - -	394	134	43	6	8	73	80	1	0	46
27 Nov. - -	523	145	74	8	7	106	98	0	1	66
4 Dec. - -	503	136	77	8	1	95	93	1	0	69
11 Dec. - -	531	147	76	9	5	95	92	0	0	83
18 Dec. - -	474	147	82	8	2	73	93	1	5	59
25 Dec. - -	374	91	56	4	2	71	62	0	0	48

TABLE II.—*continued.*

WEEKLY BILLS of MORTALITY. 1765.	Whole Number buried.	Under two Years.	Above fixty Years.	Apoplexy, Palfy, Suddenly.	Childbed and Mifcar-riage.	Confump-tion.	Fever.	Colic, Fiux, Gripes, Loofenefs.	Meafles.	Small Pox.
1 Jan. - -	511	150	74	10	7	91	92	3	0	72
8 Jan. - -	517	151	89	8	3	109	83	0	0	60
15 Jan. - -	485	157	72	5	5	96	76	2	3	48
22 Jan. - -	482	142	73	6	1	91	89	0	0	70
29 Jan. - -	423	113	65	3	1	75	71	1	0	55
5 Feb. - -	435	147	71	3	3	85	63	0	1	50
12 Feb. - -	527	159	93	5	6	100	92	0	2	43
19 Feb. - -	532	174	91	8	6	84	98	1	0	51
26 Feb. - -	655	196	103	7	9	114	106	1	5	58
5 Mar. - -	531	178	96	8	3	120	94	1	0	48
12 Mar. - -	496	202	78	5	5	118	81	0	0	44
19 Mar. - -	558	157	96	2	8	100	88	0	1	59
26 Mar. - -	534	158	86	12	7	107	96	1	0	39
2 Apr. - -	432	112	78	7	9	81	62	0	1	42
9 Apr. - -	373	126	51	3	7	67	53	1	1	27
16 Apr. - -	440	89	65	5	1	92	83	2	0	29
23 Apr. - -	409	129	64	3	6	82	76	0	1	33
30 Apr. - -	421	132	75	8	5	69	83	0	0	34
7 May - -	369	127	55	0	3	85	71	1	1	18
14 May - -	322	118	35	3	5	56	55	1	0	24
21 May - -	409	157	62	3	4	74	61	0	2	31
28 May - -	398	118	57	3	3	80	82	0	1	25
4 June - -	322	107	46	1	3	69	56	1	1	26
11 June - -	412	139	59	11	3	86	70	0	1	24
18 June - -	357	130	51	4	5	63	59	0	0	39
25 June - -	417	141	68	4	5	85	72	1	0	38

TABLE II.—*continued.*

Weekly Bills of Mortality. ——— 1765.	Whole Number buried.	Under two Years.	Above fixty Years.	Apoplexy, Palfy, Suddenly.	Childbed and Mifcar-riage.	Confump-tion.	Fever.	Colic, Flux, Gripes, Loofenefs.	Meafles.	Small Pox.
2 July - -	322	125	48	5	6	52	48	0	2	40
9 July - -	390	125	50	7	5	88	62	1	0	31
16 July - -	315	126	38	3	2	62	48	1	2	35
23 July - -	377	134	56	5	5	67	56	2	0	44
30 July - -	352	144	32	4	6	57	62	1	3	47
6 Aug. - -	357	139	43	4	1	54	67	1	3	43
13 Aug. - -	364	154	54	5	8	44	80	5	1	50
20 Aug. - -	381	162	43	7	1	42	75	2	1	51
27 Aug. - -	487	198	68	7	10	65	87	3	1	67
3 Sept. - -	451	179	50	3	10	63	72	1	0	70
10 Sept. - -	479	232	45	8	6	68	58	4	0	68
17 Sept. - -	478	215	60	3	2	84	66	2	0	52
24 Sept. - -	464	232	52	5	4	69	63	3	2	47
1 Oct. - -	498	216	57	7	9	82	80	4	2	47
8 Oct. - -	507	230	53	2	5	75	64	5	1	70
15 Oct. - -	480	202	43	1	6	86	78	4	1	72
22 Oct. - -	469	184	61	2	3	76	78	2	2	56
29 Oct. - -	428	139	55	4	4	96	74	0	0	65
5 Nov. - -	450	152	69	10	3	74	72	0	2	46
12 Nov. - -	478	157	77	5	3	81	86	2	1	47
19 Nov. - -	511	148	90	9	6	91	82	1	1	66
26 Nov. - -	500	188	69	6	2	88	80	2	0	59
3 Dec. - -	513	174	71	9	9	103	70	0	0	57
10 Dec. - -	564	171	88	5	7	106	85	0	3	73
17 Dec. - -	516	154	75	7	2	102	74	0	1	68
24 Dec. - -	500	148	87	12	3	101	77	1	1	54
31 Dec. - -	577	169	115	9	11	112	77	2	2	50

TABLE II.—*continued.*

WEEKLY BILLS of MORTALITY. 1766.	Whole Number buried.	Under two Years.	Above sixty Years.	Apoplexy, Palsy, Suddenly.	Childbed and Miscarriage.	Consumption.	Fever.	Colic, Flux, Gripes, Loosenefs.	Meafles.	Small Pox.
7 Jan, - -	546	186	111	8	7	109	79	1	3	64
14 Jan. - -	520	184	79	7	5	102	72	2	1	50
21 Jan. - -	560	158	97	12	5	105	75	1	0	60
28 Jan. - -	598	166	127	7	4	118	79	2	1	67
4 Feb. - -	530	136	103	9	2	102	90	0	1	58
11 Feb. - -	560	188	88	10	7	110	78	1	1	58
18 Feb. - -	522	178	93	9	7	103	65	1	3	51
25 Feb. - -	514	151	93	7	1	83	93	1	4	56
4 Mar. - -	471	156	75	5	3	101	61	1	8	45
11 Mar. - -	473	139	81	3	3	112	68	1	7	49
18 Mar. - -	495	167	80	6	4	95	80	1	5	54
25 Mar. - -	510	159	66	3	5	103	82	0	11	62
1 Apr. - -	485	148	71	5	8	94	63	0	12	54
8 Apr. - -	589	176	103	6	9	126	84	0	11	67
15 Apr. - -	491	187	57	6	4	90	85	1	13	59
22 Apr. - -	480	158	74	8	4	88	60	2	14	69
29 Apr. - -	431	149	66	8	1	77	63	1	9	56
6 May - -	439	127	68	4	3	95	73	0	4	51
13 May - -	401	135	55	2	1	75	74	1	15	44
20 May - -	528	180	78	7	5	106	95	4	16	51
27 May - -	428	136	62	6	6	83	69	0	16	38
3 June - -	453	138	69	5	2	83	64	1	24	53
10 June - -	449	142	59	3	5	83	79	0	25	56
17 June - -	393	155	40	1	5	78	47	0	24	39
24 June - -	368	136	47	3	6	69	49	2	15	45
1 July - -	433	136	63	13	7	84	64	0	13	53

TABLE II.—*continued.*

WEEKLY BILLS of MORTALITY. 1766.	Whole Number buried.	Under two Years.	Above fixty Years.	Apoplexy, Palfy, Suddenly	Childbed and Mifcarriage.	Confumption.	Fever.	Colic, Flux, Gripes, Loofenefs.	Meafles.	Small Pox.
8 July - -	391	149	52	7	2	65	64	0	24	25
15 July - -	374	121	51	5	0	67	61	0	29	33
22 July - -	381	126	62	6	3	76	52	1	14	37
29 July - -	340	124	38	8	1	69	39	1	13	38
5 Aug. - -	404	179	44	6	4	72	56	0	18	38
12 Aug. - -	385	139	49	4	6	76	54	3	15	34
19 Aug. - -	325	111	44	4	2	70	40	1	11	27
26 Aug. - -	337	132	47	3	4	62	59	0	5	23
2 Sept. - -	351	138	45	5	1	63	67	1	8	36
9 Sept. - -	363	150	38	6	5	64	61	1	9	28
16 Sept. - -	444	165	59	9	2	75	78	2	7	26
23 Sept. - -	393	148	52	6	4	77	54	3	11	34
30 Sept. - -	365	140	41	4	0	68	72	3	3	19
7 Oct. - -	486	217	71	2	9	98	65	1	2	43
14 Oct. - -	462	166	66	4	6	100	78	2	6	24
21 Oct. - -	436	172	55	2	6	94	63	5	6	22
28 Oct. - -	374	144	51	5	1	79	60	2	7	27
4 Nov. - -	403	142	64	7	4	78	69	1	1	24
11 Nov. - -	399	158	66	6	4	75	68	1	9	26
18 Nov. - -	483	135	58	2	2	90	91	3	4	48
25 Nov. - -	459	148	63	3	4	92	84	1	4	36
2 Dec. - -	416	131	64	6	11	85	75	4	4	27
9 Dec. - -	427	134	69	7	3	94	76	0	6	31
16 Dec. - -	454	124	66	1	5	107	76	1	6	35
23 Dec. - -	386	120	55	5	8	88	58	1	3	35
30 Dec. - -	445	114	76	4	2	106	72	1	5	32

TABLE II.—*continued.*

Weekly Bills of Mortality. 1767.	Whole Number buried.	Under two Years.	Above fixty Years.	Apoplexy, Palfy, Suddenly.	Childbed and Mifcar-riage.	Confump-tion.	Fever.	Colic, Flux, Gripes, Loofenefs.	Meafles.	Small Pox.
6 Jan. - -	391	113	69	6	7	93	51	0	4	43
13 Jan. - -	532	144	92	11	5	120	87	0	10	38
20 Jan. - -	519	129	100	16	6	126	63	2	1	42
27 Jan. - -	503	136	94	12	4	107	81	1	1	33
3 Feb. - -	468	127	84	8	2	107	76	2	0	31
10 Feb. - -	446	108	72	6	3	96	79	0	2	25
17 Feb. - -	439	137	80	5	3	101	80	1	0	18
24 Feb. - ·	413	111	67	7	3	102	61	0	0	24
3 Mar. - -	404	134	69	7	4	96	59	1	1	22
10 Mar. - -	416	144	67	9	3	86	62	0	0	21
17 Mar. · -	457	140	73	9	5	90	86	0	0	20
24 Mar. - -	439	148	64	10	5	105	65	0	0	27
31 Mar. - -	432	162	71	5	3	86	59	1	1	24
7 Apr. - -	472	177	70	2	8	88	79	1	1	25
14 Apr. - -	392	126	53	7	3	75	72	2	3	16
21 Apr. - -	419	137	60	3	4	90	70	1	1	35
28 Apr. - -	519	205	58	10	6	109	73	5	2	28
5 May - -	462	167	79	8	2	90	69	1	1	29
12 May - -	441	158	65	4	1	78	61	0	3	49
19 May - -	448	153	70	6	3	96	69	1	3	39
26 May - -	422	142	75	2	3	87	75	0	2	36
2 June - -	385	139	56	7	2	80	62	0	0	39
9 June - -	408	142	66	3	5	84	61	0	3	41
16 June - -	423	146	57	3	4	68	72	0	2	38
23 June - -	431	146	56	6	1	87	57	1	1	48
30 June - -	457	149	78	7	4	85	70	2	2	51

TABLE II.—*continued.*

WEEKLY BILLS of MORTALITY. 1767.	Whole Number buried.	Under two years.	Above sixty years.	Apoplexy, Palsy, Suddenly.	Childbed and Miscarriage.	Consumption.	Fever.	Colic, Flux, Gripes, Looseness.	Measles.	Small Pox.
7 July - -	476	129	81	5	4	86	95	1	1	49
14 July - -	358	128	37	4	3	61	71	3	0	29
21 July - -	398	131	54	8	3	81	71	1	0	46
28 July - -	399	120	73	3	5	57	83	1	1	42
4 Aug. - -	339	102	40	7	3	64	53	4	1	47
11 Aug. - -	407	136	59	8	4	77	71	1	1	51
18 Aug. - -	350	108	43	3	2	59	70	1	1	58
25 Aug. - -	371	160	51	2	0	52	68	3	0	44
1 Sept. - -	352	140	43	5	0	60	40	3	1	43
8 Sept. - -	384	138	37	6	4	60	67	4	0	54
15 Sept. - -	338	144	36	4	2	48	56	2	1	47
22 Sept. - -	358	145	56	5	2	57	52	1	0	55
29 Sept. - -	388	165	42	3	1	62	70	4	1	42
6 Oct. - -	444	184	43	4	1	99	62	9	0	54
13 Oct. - -	469	177	57	4	3	75	78	2	4	44
20 Oct. - -	437	196	57	10	2	69	64	6	2	54
27 Oct. - -	396	134	49	3	4	61	73	0	1	64
3 Nov. - -	564	229	69	2	4	96	91	1	5	64
10 Nov. - -	450	176	55	7	1	72	78	0	0	59
17 Nov. - -	446	157	52	6	2	77	83	1	0	67
24 Nov. - -	487	173	54	2	2	80	84	0	2	61
1 Dec. - -	544	176	82	6	7	110	110	3	3	57
8 Dec. - -	475	160	67	13	5	93	91	0	1	48
15 Dec. - -	613	206	80	6	4	101	113	1	2	109
22 Dec. - -	495	157	62	4	5	76	97	0	2	74
29 Dec. - -	441	195	63	5	2	94	77	2	2	61

D

TABLE II.—*continued.*

WEEKLY BILLS of MORTALITY. 1795.	Whole Number buried.	Under two years.	Above fixty years.	Apoplexy, Palfy, Suddenly.	Childbed and Mifcar- riage.	Confump- tion.	Fever.	Colic, Flux, Gripes, Loofenefs.	Meafles.	Small Pox.
6 Jan. - -	244	66	51	4	1	73	20	0	5	17
13 Jan. - -	532	129	139	13	6	158	49	0	9	14
20 Jan. - -	637	141	145	11	5	164	81	2	9	17
27 Jan. - -	543	128	143	11	5	157	42	0	3	24
3 Feb. - -	867	153	239	13	5	273	66	0	4	18
10 Feb. - -	735	133	203	11	6	231	55	0	5	21
17 Feb. - -	678	148	171	7	4	198	61	1	4	13
24 Feb. - -	635	145	150	12	8	155	49	1	9	19
3 Mar. - -	687	169	168	6	5	202	63	0	7	9
10 Mar. - -	568	155	131	6	3	142	54	1	4	5
17 Mar. - -	540	158	102	7	2	161	45	0	8	14
24 Mar. - -	446	146	82	4	5	111	41	0	5	9
31 Mar. - -	483	164	89	7	4	128	34	0	4	8
7 Apr. - -	339	111	65	6	1	97	35	0	3	5
14 Apr. - -	491	166	84	5	2	125	43	1	4	6
21 Apr. - -	426	146	54	3	3	127	48	1	10	5
28 Apr. - -	462	143	71	2	3	129	42	0	4	3
5 May - -	427	150	81	7	3	113	27	1	5	9
12 May - -	365	135	45	3	0	109	37	0	4	5
19 May - -	441	139	64	5	4	120	40	0	13	18
26 May - -	303	95	43	10	2	102	21	0	0	3
2 June - -	419	124	62	2	6	128	41	1	3	9
9 June - -	348	111	57	2	2	89	38	0	5	15
16 June - -	341	87	63	9	3	105	35	1	4	14
23 June - -	281	83	48	8	3	99	26	0	4	9
30 June - -	342	105	43	3	4	98	34	0	5	18

TABLE II.—*continued.*

WEEKLY BILLS of MORTALITY. 1795.	Whole Number buried.	Under two Years.	Above fixty Years.	Apoplexy, Palfy, Suddenly.	Childbed and Mifcar-riage.	Confump-tion.	Fever.	Colic, Flux, Gripes, Loofenefs.	Meafles.	Small Pox.
7 July - -	245	72	41	5	1	68	30	0	5	13
14 July - -	362	86	63	12	0	92	39	0	5	23
21 July - -	273	95	42	8	2	95	28	0	6	16
28 July - -	303	108	42	3	2	89	29	0	6	25
4 Aug. - -	225	79	30	4	1	66	22	0	6	14
11 Aug. - -	193	59	24	1	3	51	24	0	0	15
18 Aug. - -	266	91	32	3	1	59	35	0	4	15
25 Aug. - -	232	74	34	3	0	62	24	0	1	11
1 Sept. - -	266	104	36	4	1	50	25	0	9	23
8 Sept. - -	398	172	57	4	3	81	31	0	3	21
15 Sept. - -	281	121	28	6	1	58	32	1	14	11
22 Sept. - -	247	113	24	2	2	42	16	1	6	23
29 Sept. - -	311	142	37	4	1	79	27	1	3	27
6 Oct. - -	410	184	58	7	5	90	26	1	16	28
13 Oct. - -	321	129	42	4	5	60	38	1	12	23
20 Oct. - -	360	151	39	4	1	79	43	1	8	47
27 Oct. - -	340	120	34	4	2	73	37	1	12	41
3 Nov. - -	320	129	34	3	0	82	28	1	14	27
10 Nov. - -	351	132	51	4	1	68	33	1	7	52
17 Nov. - -	595	186	76	5	5	175	47	0	15	67
24 Nov. - -	276	92	33	4	2	73	24	0	8	29
1 Dec. - -	691	193	103	5	3	204	56	0	7	62
8 Dec. - -	497	185	82	3	1	112	49	0	8	75
15 Dec. - -	233	67	39	5	1	61	27	0	11	28
22 Dec. - -	340	131	46	6	4	82	28	1	15	68
29 Dec. - -	253	70	26	2	3	56	27	0	11	47

TABLE II.—*continued.*

WEEKLY BILLS of MORTALITY. 1796.	Whole Number buried.	Under two Years.	Above sixty Years.	Apoplexy, Palsy, Suddenly.	Childbed and Miscar-riage.	Consump-tion.	Fever.	Colic, Flux, Gripes, Loosenefs.	Measles.	Small Pox.
5 Jan. - -	300	100	35	7	5	79	34	o	3	42
12 Jan. - -	273	87	37	5	1	53	25	1	9	32
19 Jan. - -	313	113	29	4	2	77	29	o	o	51
26 Jan. - -	257	96	20	11	2	47	23	o	1	44
2 Feb. - -	328	110	32	6	1	86	23	o	10	36
9 Feb. - -	363	122	44	7	6	93	33	o	4	62
16 Feb. - -	329	123	41	4	2	89	21	o	5	43
23 Feb. - -	372	119	65	6	3	90	31	o	7	51
1 Mar. - -	339	125	48	4	2	86	20	o	3	39
8 Mar. - -	323	112	45	6	2	91	17	o	6	47
15 Mar. - -	384	129	48	7	4	92	24	o	10	47
22 Mar. - -	363	130	48	6	2	92	30	o	4	33
29 Mar. - -	293	97	38	8	o	76	19	o	3	33
5 Apr. - -	415	147	57	4	3	116	28	c	5	50
12 Apr. - -	420	134	64	7	6	92	29	o	3	45
19 Apr. - -	366	146	42	3	3	84	22	o	4	44
26 Apr. - -	400	136	65	6	3	96	22	1	5	52
3 May - -	312	105	49	3	6	72	19	o	3	49
10 May - -	334	128	38	1	3	67	27	o	4	60
17 May - -	328	95	55	10	3	71	29	o	3	55
24 May - -	375	141	39	5	2	69	35	o	6	90
31 May - -	382	112	46	3	6	92	35	o	5	77
7 June - -	378	140	43	4	4	86	34	1	o	83
14 June - -	320	122	28	2	1	70	20	o	o	96
21 June - -	333	112	39	5	4	60	31	o	4	88
28 June - -	318	115	42	5	4	61	20	o	11	73

TABLE II.—*continued.*

WEEKLY BILLS of MORTALITY. 1796.	Whole Number buried.	Under two Years.	Above fixty Years.	Between twenty and fifty Years.	Apoplexy, Palfy, Suddenly.	Confump-tion.	Fever.	Convul-fions.	Afthma.	Dropfy.
5 July - -	328	105	32	59	6	60	16	46	4	12
12 July - -	402	129	40	98	7	81	40	69	1	10
19 July - -	384	122	46	71	7	69	32	64	12	11
26 July - -	342	116	40	77	7	61	35	60	0	12
2 Aug. - -	324	116	30	80	2	80	17	57	6	12
9 Aug. - -	346	141	36	62	9	61	19	59	2	6
16 Aug. - -	306	119	25	69	5	62	19	49	1	8
23 Aug. - -	285	111	31	51	4	47	15	55	2	8
30 Aug. - -	373	140	35	78	3	75	34	73	6	22
6 Sept. - -	368	147	34	80	7	65	29	88	2	12
13 Sept. - -	447	185	48	85	6	91	36	83	4	13
20 Sept. - -	316	128	26	55	5	54	28	44	1	11
27 Sept. - -	433	184	47	74	2	60	48	79	8	18
4 Oct. - -	366	144	39	58	6	62	19	73	1	12
11 Oct. - -	411	160	45	86	5	77	31	86	6	10
18 Oct. - -	303	139	35	57	7	67	26	63	3	7
25 Oct. - -	332	120	43	83	5	68	35	66	1	16
1 Nov. - -	424	136	68	96	8	96	36	74	6	21
8 Nov. - -	416	149	45	101	8	104	30	101	2	16
15 Nov. - -	444	145	61	113	4	113	46	82	9	15
22 Nov. - -	295	106	33	81	7	69	25	64	9	19
29 Nov. - -	383	140	63	91	9	80	38	90	12	19
6 Dec. - -	293	80	45	89	4	70	27	48	4	2
13 Dec. - -	1223*	342	226	332	16	309	95	275	47	29
20 Dec. - -	257	93	38	65	4	66	22	49	11	9
27 Dec. - -	206	64	35	51	3	65	20	46	7	9

* The Parifh of St. George, Middlefex, gave in the Number for the whole Year, amountirg to 532.

TABLE II.—*continued.*

WEEKLY BILLS of MORTALITY. 1797.	Whole Number buried.	Under two Years.	Above fixty Years.	Between twenty and fifty Years.	Apoplexy, Palfy, Suddenly.	Confump-tion.	Fever.	Convul-fions.	Afthma.	Dropfy.
3 Jan. - -	544	161	90	148	14	147	45	105	16	23
10 Jan. - -	438	118	82	108	7	127	41	79	22	17
17 Jan. - -	290	87	63	71	5	73	31	55	13	13
24 Jan. - -	435	133	85	117	9	135	43	75	17	14
31 Jan. - -	421	134	82	110	10	118	31	72	20	24
7 Feb. - -	341	97	62	85	9	92	27	71	15	10
14 Feb. - -	304	78	53	85	7	104	31	54	9	10
21 Feb. - -	367	103	66	99	7	116	26	77	18	15
28 Feb. - -	393	108	81	104	5	102	33	77	21	21
7 Mar. - -	491	117	111	144	10	139	45	86	31	18
14 Mar. - -	412	109	104	103	8	116	30	78	27	20
21 Mar. - -	387	83	104	113	12	111	26	66	29	22
28 Mar. - -	508	113	126	139	9	151	39	99	30	30
4 Apr. - -	371	103	82	91	7	114	29	75	15	20
11 Apr. - -	309	80	53	92	9	73	32	63	15	15
18 Apr. - -	326	103	52	79	3	97	33	80	5	13
25 Apr. - -	371	105	59	121	3	101	31	82	30	20
2 May - -	362	92	78	105	9	110	35	78	14	17
9 May - -	300	85	43	91	3	92	31	62	8	14
16 May - -	328	92	54	94	5	105	22	73	3	16
23 May - -	309	78	46	102	7	92	22	54	2	30
30 May - -	271	73	47	77	6	73	24	67	3	15
6 June - -	265	82	38	72	6	75	28	61	3	9
13 June - -	257	66	46	79	2	77	18	63	6	11
20 June - -	326	97	49	96	7	99	35	67	3	18
27 June - -	256	69	40	82	3	85	22	64	1	16

TABLE II.—*continued.*

WEEKLY BILLS of MORTALITY. 1797.	Whole Number buried.	Under two Years.	Above fixty Years.	Between twenty and fifty Years.	Apoplexy, Palfy, Suddenly.	Confump-tion.	Fever.	Convul-fions.	Afthma.	Dropfy.
4 July - -	292	86	46	87	4	90	24	60	5	19
11 July - -	236	77	27	70	4	71	20	48	4	14
18 July - -	274	76	48	92	1	94	22	48	2	12
25 July - -	192	57	23	59	6	38	22	48	3	16
1 Aug. - -	289	98	38	74	7	79	24	74	1	10
8 Aug. - -	243	78	44	66	3	69	25	65	2	10
15 Aug. - -	333	112	45	91	5	92	35	83	7	14
22 Aug. - -	247	96	32	65	3	63	22	76	4	9
29 Aug. - -	263	107	30	70	7	47	24	73	2	13
5 Sept. - -	262	120	28	54	6	44	21	95	1	8
12 Sept. - -	261	92	35	78	2	65	28	69	9	15
19 Sept. - -	288	112	44	68	3	65	24	77	6	18
26 Sept. - -	289	117	41	63	9	65	24	90	3	9
3 Oct. - -	264	94	33	79	3	54	36	63	5	20
10 Oct. - -	255	81	44	66	3	60	24	65	6	11
17 Oct. - -	293	83	28	101	6	81	38	73	5	13
24 Oct. - -	206	81	31	52	2	56	17	53	1	13
31 Oct. - -	304	92	47	88	6	68	31	64	14	13
7 Nov. - -	360	119	60	83	6	96	26	92	1	13
14 Nov. - -	263	78	43	81	6	71	22	65	9	22
21 Nov. - -	383	107	47	123	4	108	42	85	13	13
28 Nov. - -	337	118	55	92	6	99	19	99	4	18
5 Dec. - -	422	115	63	122	8	130	45	102	13	27
12 Dec. - -	625	180	107	159	11	204	50	159	14	33
19 Dec. - -	180	49	33	56	7	53	10	42	6	15
26 Dec. - -	205	64	36	63	2	50	18	41	6	12

TABLE II.—*continued.*

WEEKLY BILLS of MORTALITY. 1798.	Whole Number buried.	Under two Years.	Above sixty Years.	Between twenty and fifty Years.	Apoplexy, Palfy, Suddenly.	Confump- tion.	Fever.	Convul- fions.	Afthma.	Dropfy.
2 Jan. - -	349	119	41	86	7	100	23	91	8	18
9 Jan. - -	280	78	38	81	10	77	25	69	13	15
16 Jan. - -	396	114	83	103	8	93	39	99	14	16
23 Jan. - -	295	83	54	82	14	84	28	69	12	15
30 Jan. - -	305	104	45	83	6	93	24	81	9	14
6 Feb. - -	314	81	63	86	10	91	23	63	8	22
13 Feb. - -	405	120	68	102	5	109	40	88	13	22
20 Feb. - -	391	100	78	127	6	116	44	69	16	23
27 Feb. - -	495	132	96	138	9	133	33	109	17	30
6 Mar. - -	403	112	68	114	9	125	27	88	16	22
13 Mar. - -	320	95	63	75	7	99	18	68	12	14
20 Mar. - -	328	102	48	102	10	96	28	67	18	24
27 Mar. - -	380	120	68	106	4	119	29	96	12	20
3 Apr. - -	360	115	51	101	6	112	27	87	11	15
10 Apr. - -	252	76	39	62	3	69	27	47	9	18
17 Apr. - -	415	131	51	111	5	122	31	95	10	18
24 Apr. - -	340	94	40	106	6	84	44	62	9	18
1 May - -	372	95	58	113	10	98	29	72	10	19
8 May - -	304	80	38	92	3	90	19	78	7	14
15 May - -	349	99	44	109	6	99	33	54	11	14
22 May - -	308	89	38	91	10	88	25	59	3	19
29 May - -	266	72	37	72	4	69	33	40	7	18
5 June - -	329	97	47	99	5	81	29	58	7	12
12 June - -	346	104	47	104	2	96	39	68	5	11
19 June - -	321	87	45	94	6	80	29	69	5	12
26 June - -	349	112	49	99	5	92	34	72	5	10

TABLE II.—*continued.*

WEEKLY BILLS of MORTALITY. 1798.	Whole Number buried.	Under two Years.	Above fixty Years.	Between twenty and fifty Years.	Apoplexy, Palfy, Suddenly.	Confumption.	Fever.	Convulfions.	Afthma.	Dropfy.
3 July - -	308	96	44	82	2	71	29	58	5	10
10 July - -	267	78	45	66	6	66	30	48	5	11
17 July - -	329	98	47	77	4	96	33	49	5	14
24 July - -	335	121	35	93	4	86	30	67	7	9
31 July - -	396	149	48	91	11	65	37	80	5	10
7 Aug. - -	329	118	40	77	7	83	35	86	2	12
14 Aug. - -	302	114	47	62	3	58	30	73	3	12
21 Aug. - -	387	151	46	90	5	73	39	73	6	18
28 Aug. - -	311	114	39	69	8	54	28	65	0	19
4 Sept. - -	358	144	33	72	9	80	39	85	6	8
11 Sept. - -	372	159	39	73	1	90	34	78	6	10
18 Sept. - -	432	188	57	75	3	88	29	108	10	13
25 Sept. - -	341	122	46	72	9	60	42	62	2	15
2 Oct. - -	416	141	32	101	3	86	56	70	6	12
9 Oct. - -	311	121	37	59	2	54	34	58	4	12
16 Oct. - -	333	107	42	85	4	70	42	55	5	11
23 Oct. - -	422	133	58	104	8	98	45	74	4	16
30 Oct. - -	300	93	45	70	3	59	40	52	1	7
6 Nov. - -	422	117	56	102	8	106	39	68	8	15
13 Nov. - -	353	112	31	80	4	86	42	53	7	16
20 Nov. - -	334	105	46	90	5	83	37	50	9	10
27 Nov. - -	403	116	62	98	8	89	56	75	11	7
4 Dec. - -	556	160	89	128	5	116	59	100	5	19
11 Dec. - -	481	147	67	117	10	98	49	75	20	17
18 Dec. - -	395	118	57	88	4	89	49	79	18	10
25 Dec. - -	448	120	86	110	3	127	52	90	7	12

E

TABLE II.—*continued.*

WEEKLY BILLS of MORTALITY. 1799.	Whole Number buried.	Under two Years.	Above fixty Years.	Between twenty and fifty Years.	Apoplexy, Palfy, Suddenly.	Confumption.	Fever.	Convulfions.	Afthma.	Dropfy.
1 Jan. - -	364	107	72	91	10	98	40	59	9	14
8 Jan. - -	458	161	69	104	4	107	50	92	18	16
15 Jan. - -	478	137	88	135	6	113	32	90	28	26
22 Jan. - -	496	127	86	153	3	128	60	82	38	25
29 Jan. - -	408	129	70	103	7	90	41	88	21	7
5 Feb. - -	395	103	86	105	10	93	32	75	26	18
12 Feb. - -	479	147	86	135	8	130	48	115	20	20
19 Feb. - -	494	135	85	133	7	140	45	91	38	26
26 Feb. - -	429	117	85	116	9	88	44	73	33	11
5 Mar. - -	385	110	71	97	8	106	29	69	26	15
12 Mar. - -	339	84	73	86	9	88	38	71	15	14
19 Mar. - -	329	86	56	94	11	97	23	62	11	21
26 Mar. - -	291	80	47	84	5	73	29	63	11	13
2 Apr. - -	433	102	94	120	9	148	32	84	21	23
9 Apr. - -	434	125	83	115	5	126	48	109	11	23
16 Apr. - -	431	113	93	105	11	118	30	88	24	21
23 Apr. - -	267	76	42	82	6	88	22	74	12	9
30 Apr. - -	395	119	63	113	8	115	42	95	13	24
7 May - -	280	86	53	80	3	75	22	67	6	13
14 May - -	244	53	39	90	0	71	37	46	13	16
21 May - -	472	132	116	117	14	145	25	107	15	25
28 May - -	398	108	81	104	6	114	39	81	14	22
4 June - -	301	88	59	79	4	97	24	66	6	14
11 June - -	284	90	50	69	7	76	18	65	8	17
18 June - -	236	61	51	81	3	69	33	49	10	15
25 June - -	321	96	51	99	4	98	36	65	12	23

TABLE II.—*continued.*

WEEKLY BILLS of MORTALITY. 1799.	Whole Number buried.	Under two Years.	Above fixty Years.	Between twenty and fifty Years.	Apoplexy, Palfy, Suddenly.	Confump-tion.	Fever.	Convul-fions.	Afthma.	Dropfy.
2 July - -	262	66	57	71	7	74	27	58	10	18
9 July - -	271	69	50	86	5	83	35	40	3	18
16 July - -	321	66	63	98	11	87	29	63	6	25
23 July - -	263	85	49	71	6	64	19	60	3	19
30 July - -	200	72	31	54	2	55	20	50	2	13
6 Aug. - -	300	90	52	85	9	87	25	69	7	16
13 Aug. - -	297	89	43	72	5	80	24	77	5	12
20 Aug. - -	248	74	38	64	10	67	25	51	7	12
27 Aug. - -	184	62	27	43	3	56	16	49	6	7
3 Sept. - -	275	79	56	72	6	69	29	63	7	9
10 Sept. - -	231	72	27	73	5	59	21	56	0	20
17 Sept. - -	212	64	34	50	6	49	27	31	8	12
24 Sept. - -	296	84	43	79	5	86	37	67	7	18
1 Oct. - -	255	90	37	65	2	62	34	55	4	13
8 Oct. - -	394	124	46	118	8	119	33	109	2	18
15 Oct. - -	318	88	35	110	3	81	51	60	4	16
22 Oct. - -	292	93	47	74	9	76	33	70	3	11
29 Oct. - -	310	104	45	85	7	86	35	70	6	16
5 Nov. - -	298	88	53	81	7	56	35	68	9	17
12 Nov. - -	337	98	57	95	6	85	35	76	7	25
19 Nov. - -	284	81	47	89	9	80	23	53	6	12
26 Nov. - -	409	133	62	103	12	112	34	72	13	23
3 Dec. - -	389	122	79	86	11	88	34	84	14	19
10 Dec. - -	786	207	140	235	14	175	78	158	40	44
17 Dec. - -	272	72	47	64	4	73	24	40	19	18
24 Dec. - -	318	79	55	97	10	79	40	58	23	17
31 Dec. - -	358	108	70	89	6	100	31	79	10	24

PART I.

OF THE

INCREASE AND DECREASE.

OF

DIFFERENT DISEASES.

THE fluctuation obfervable in certain difeafes may be confidered under two diftinct points of view: the firft comprehending their variations in different years ; the fecond thofe which take place in different parts of the fame year. Each of them affords matter of curiofity, and ufeful information.

THE two preceding Tables exhibit a method in which fuch obfervations may fafely be conducted. For, whatever errors be fuppofed to have crept into the regifters from which they are formed, yet when taken together, and confidered on an extenfive fcale, they muft be admitted to conftitute a very unexceptionable bafis for medical reafoning. And the feveral objects being thus brought nearer to each other, and feen as it were fide by fide, the judgment may be formed not only much more eafily, but, it is apprehended, much more certainly alfo, than could be done in any other manner. Another

great

great advantage refulting from fuch tables is, that they do of themfelves often fuggeft conclufions, which correct, or perhaps wholly contradict, the expectations raifed upon no better foundation than vague conjecture, or popular opinion.

THE particular articles, of which thefe tables are compofed, were felected as being thofe from which moft was expected to be learned. It fhould however be noticed, that the weekly table is not perfectly uniform; for, inftead of being made out from ten years in fucceffion, five were chofen at one time, and five others after an interval of above thirty years : to afford an opportunity of comparing the two periods with each other. Befides, from July 1796, an alteration may be obferved in the mode of keeping them. But this, which was introduced to fatisfy fome views of the author, it is hoped will rather prove an advantage, than any embarrafsment, to thofe who may be inclined to examine it; and therefore has not fince been changed.

1. OF the variation in the whole numbers chriftened and buried.

THE annual mortality appears by the parifh clerks returns to have increafed from the beginning of the century to the year 1720; to have been at its greateft height from 1720 to 1750; and from that time gradually to have decreafed.

IN the mean' time, the chriftenings increafed from 1700 to 1727; then decreafed to 1740; were at the loweft between

1740

1740 and 1760; and from that time have gradually increafed.

THAT both the chriftenings and burials fhould have become more frequent during the firft thirty years, can be no
matter of furprife, when we confider the increafe both in
number, and fize, of the out-parifhes. For it will be found
upon examination, that the increafe has been confined to
them alone.

ON the other hand, the fubfequent decreafe of burials
has taken place only in the city parifhes; and is, no doubt,
owing to people living wider, and taking up more room than
formerly. They no longer fubmit to the inconvenience of
being crowded feveral together under a fingle roof. But
many merchants with their families, and many merchants'
clerks alfo, who ufed all to live in the fame houfe, now retire,
efpecially when they are fick, to others fituated without the
limits of the bills of mortality, or at leaft without the city.

IN the firft five years of the century, the average numbers
dying annually in each of the four divifions into which the
parifhes are diftributed, were as follows:

Within the Walls.	Without the Walls.	Out Parifhes.	Weftminfter.
2,192	6,873	6,223	3,285

between the years 1740 and 1745 they were

2,328	6,975	11,784	6,164

and from 1790 to 1795 they were

1,374	4,108	9,600	5,110

AND

And though London has been very much extended, and the number of its inhabitants proportionally enlarged within the laſt thirty years; yet this having taken place principally in the pariſh of Mary-le-bone, which is not included in the bills of mortality, it therefore makes no addition to the yearly accounts.

It is not eaſy to account for the diminution of chriſtenings between the years 1740 and 1760. But it may be obſerved, that the number of females buried in the ſame twenty years not being ſenſibly leſſened, the defect, however that ſhould happen, ſeems to have ariſen from the ſmaller proportion among them who bore children.

Whatever be the cauſe of this, the chriſtenings appear in fact to have been feweſt at a time when the burials were nearly at the higheſt. Hence the difference of the numbers chriſtened and buried is greater between the years 1740 and 1750, than at any preceding or ſubſequent period. This difference diminiſhed afterwards; but ſtill continued very conſiderable till about 1770. Now, it was from an average of ten years taken in this interval, namely from 1759 to 1768, that Dr. Price conſtructed his (a) tables of the probabilities of life, and from which he deduced the population of London. The exceſs of the burials above the chriſtenings amounted at that time to nearly one-third (b) of the whole number

(a) Tab. XIII. and XV. of his Obſervations on Reverſionary Payments, 5th edit.   (b) Vol. I. p. 340.

number of burials. At prefent, it is lefs than one-twentieth : nay, in the years 1790, 1797, and 1799, the excefs was actually on the fide of the chriftenings. Such a prodigious change ought, one would think, confiderably to alter Dr. Price's conclufions. Some allowances are however to be made (c) ; particularly in confequence of an act of parliament paffed in 1767, by which it is required that all parifh infants fhall be fent into the country in three weeks after their birth, to be nurfed there till they are fix years old. How many burials of children are taken out of the bills in confequence of this act, it is not eafy to eftimate ; but that it muft be a large number, is rendered probable by the remark-able decreafe of thofe reported to die under two years of age. Between the years 1728, when the ages were firft fet down, and 1738, their number amounted one year with another to above 10,000 ; in the next decad to above 9,000 ; in the decad following to 7,800 ; and between 1790 and 1800, to little more than 6,000 annually. It is to be hoped, however, that as this decreafe began to take place before the date of the act in queftion, fo its continuance fince may in part be with juftice attributed to the greater falubrity of the town (c*).

2. THERE

(c) See of Dr. P.'s Work, Vol. I. p. 251. note.

(c*) It appears from the books of the Foundling Hofpital, that the mortality among the children under the age of twelve months, who are all put out to nurfe in the country, has within the laft thirty years, diminifhed in the proportion of twelve to feven. The average of the laft ten years being only one in fix.

Account of Foundling Hofpital in London, 1799.

2. THERE is fcarcely any fact to be collected from the bills of mortality more worthy the attention of phyficians, than the gradual decline of the dyfentery. In the feventeenth century, the number of deaths under the titles of *bloody-flux* and *griping in the guts*, appear never to have been lefs than one thoufand, and fome years to have exceeded four thoufand; and for five and twenty years together, from 1667 to 1692, they every year amounted to above two thoufand. But from the beginning of the eighteenth century things were materially changed. After the year 1733, the article of *griping in the guts* was joined to that of *colic:* taking then the three difeafes of *bloody-flux*, *colic*, and *gripes*, we may obferve their decreafe to have been nearly as follows:

From 1700 to 1710 the average is about 1,070 annually.

1710 to 1720 - - - - - -	770
1720 to 1730 - - - - - -	700
1730 to 1740 - - - - - -	350
1740 to 1750 - - - - - -	150
1750 to 1760 - - - - - -	110
1760 to 1770 - - - - - -	80
1770 to 1780 - - - - - -	70
1780 to 1790 - - - - - -	40
1790 to 1800 - - - - - -	20

Even in the years 1762 and 1780, when modern phyficians have defcribed the dyfentery as epidemical in London, the amount of the fame three articles was in the firft year only 209, and in the laft 93.

THE

THE caufe of fo great an alteration in the health of the people of England (for it is not confined to the metropolis) I have no hefitation in attributing to the improvements which have gradually taken place, not only in London, but in all great towns, and in the manner of living throughout the kingdom; particulaily with refpect to cleanlinefs and ventilation. For the reafons upon which this opinion is founded, I muft refer the reader to what will be faid hereafter *(d)* concerning the plague.

3. The inoculation of the fmall pox having been firft ufed in England fince the beginning of the eighteenth century, and having been now for many years generally adopted by all the middle and higher orders of fociety; it becomes an interefting enquiry to obferve, from a review of the laft hundred years, what have been the effects of fo great an innovation, upon the mortality occafioned by that difeafe. But, however beneficial inoculation prove to individuals, or indeed to the nation at large, the bills of mortality inconteftibly fhew, that in London more perfons have died of the fmall pox fince the introduction of that practice.

THE poor, who have little care of preferving their lives beyond the getting their daily bread, make a very large part of mankind. Their prejudices are ftrong, and not eafily overcome by reafon. Hence, while the inoculation of the wealthy keeps up a perpetual fource of infection, many others,

who

(d) Part II.

F 2

who either cannot afford, or do not chufe, to adopt the fame method, are continually expofed to the diftemper. And the danger is ftill increafed by the inconfiderate manner in which it has lately been the cuftom to fend into the open air perfons in every ftage of the difeafe, without any regard to the fafety of their neighbours. It is by thefe means, that while inocu-lation may juftly be efteemed one of the greateft improve-ments ever introduced into the medical art, it occafions many to fall a facrifice to what has obtained the diftinction of the *natural* difeafe. This muft always be an objection againft making any great city the place for inoculation, until the practice is become univerfal among all ranks of people.

Out of every thoufand deaths in the bills of mortality, the number attributed to the fmall pox during the firft thirty years of the eighteenth century, before inoculation could yet have had any effect upon them, amounted to 74. During an equal number of years at the end of the century, they amounted to 95. So that, as far as we are enabled to judge from hence, they would appear to have increafed in a propor-tion of above five to four.

I cannot refufe myfelf the fatisfaction of ftating on the other hand, from the printed accounts of the Small Pox Hof-pital, where from their numbers the truth can beft be afcer-tained, that while by the natural fmall pox there die one in fix, from the inoculated fmall pox three hundred and ninety-nine out of four hundred recover.

4. The

4. THE yearly fum of the deaths ranged under the heads of apoplexy, palfy, and fuddenly, fluctuates without any certain increafe or decreafe till the beginning of the eighteenth century. From that time, the proportion they bear to the whole number of deaths may be obferved to have been gradually, and conftantly, increafing. It is now above double what it was an hundred years ago. To what caufe then ought this to be attributed ? Is it owing to any alteration in our manners ? or in our diet ? and what is that alteration ? Some perfons have accufed fpirituous liquors ; fome the ufe of tea ; and other things. But I confefs myfelf by no means fatisfied either with the conjectures of others, or with any I have myfelf been able to form upon this fubject. The fact however refts upon too ftrong evidence to be queftioned.

5. THE deaths imputed to the meafles are very remarkably different in different years ; fometimes amounting to one thirtieth of the whole number of deaths, and at other times falling fhort of one in four thoufand. Yet it is poffible that this difeafe may not in reality be fo very irregularly epidemical, or fatal.. The fcarlet fever, and malignant fore throat, often occafion fuch appearances upon the fkin, as may eafily be miftaken for the meafles by better judges than the mothers and nurfes, who thinking themfelves able to diftinguifh this diftemper, and equal to the management of it, often call in no other affiftance. This miftake is well known to have been fometimes committed within thefe few years, during which the fcarlet fever, and malignant fore throat, have been

fo

fo generally underſtood. It may perhaps have happened in every year, in which an extraordinary number of deaths are charged to the meaſles. If ſo, thoſe two formidable diſtempers (if indeed they are two diſtinct diſtempers, and not one and the ſame) being diſguiſed under the name of meaſles, may have been older, and more general, than is uſually imagined *(e)*.

6. The table does not repreſent the mortality among lying-in women to be diminiſhed in a degree equal to the truth. But it muſt be remembered, that the proportion dying on this account ought to be referred to the number of births, and not to the burials, as was there done for the ſake of uniformity. Eſtimated in this way, the numbers would be materially altered. As for inſtance, out of every thouſand deliveries during the firſt ten years, fifteen women would then appear to have died inſtead of eleven ; and ſo of the reſt.

The following Table is inſerted from the printed account of the Britiſh Lying-in Hoſpital in Brownlow-ſtreet, which gives a much more favourable ſtatement of this matter :

(e) No leſs an author than Morton appears to have confounded together the meaſles and the ſcarlet fever. He ſays, in his 5th chap. *De Febre Scarlatina,* " Hunc morbum prorſus eundem eſſe cum morbillis cenſeo, et ſola effloreſcentiæ " modo ab illis diſtare."

ACCOUNT of the WOMEN DELIVERED, and CHILDREN BORN, in the BRITISH LYING-IN HOSPITAL, as alfo the TWINS, STILL-BIRTHS, and DEATHS, from the Time of its Inſtitution, in November 1749, to the Firſt of January 1801 incluſive.

A. D.	No. of Women Delivered.	Boys Born.	Girls Born.	Total No. of Children Born.	Women had Twins.	Children Still-born.	Children Died.	Women Died.	PROPORTION of DEATHS.	
									Of the Women.	Of the Children.
1749	3	3		3						
1750	175	93	84	177	2	11	5	3		
1751	337	181	160	341	4	15	9	12		
1752	433	236	201	437	4	22	27	14		
1753	284	141	146	287	3	10	21	10		
1754	321	175	151	326	5	9	66	12	1 in 42	1 in 15.
1755	370	190	185	375	5	8	34	9		
1756	370	188	184	372	2	8	10	3		
1757	478	262	219	481	3	12	22	7		
1758	521	277	254	531	10	6	16	8		
1759	472	253	226	479	7	12	14	6		
1760	427	228	206	434	7	11	58	26		
1761	390	197	198	395	5	20	31	12		
1762	397	199	199	398	1	8	38	7		
1763	414	209	212	421	7	15	32	10	1 in 50	1 in 20.
1764	366	191	178	369	3	15	17	7		
1765	560	311	258	569	9	12	20	9		
1766	588	293	304	597	9	25	17	10		
1767	571	303	272	575	4	7	10	4		
1768	588	301	288	589	1	5	2	3		
1769	561	292	280	572	11	14	13	7		
1770	472	225	249	474	2	13	9	28		
1771	541	266	282	548	7	17	14	4		
1772	596	320	286	606	10	25	17	4		
1773	627	336	298	634	7	19	14	4	1 in 53	1 in 42.
1774	553	292	266	558	5	36	3	18		
1775	570	295	280	575	5	22	13	21		
1776	543	276	275	551	8	26	9	3		
1777	602	312	293	605	3	24	24	6		
1778	572	281	298	579	7	19	18	11		

A. D.	No. of Women Delivered.	Boys Born.	Girls Born.	Total No. of Children Born.	Women had Twins.	Children Still-born.	Children Died.	Women Died.	PROPORTION of DEATHS.	
									Of the Women.	Of the Children.
1779	563	310	257	567	4	31	8	3		
1780	566	310	259	569	3	33	4	8		
1781	524	275	255	530	6	26	9	14		
1782	549	298	260	558	9	15	14	13		
1783	587	308	288	596	9	33	17	5	1 in 60	1 in 44.
1784	550	283	272	555	5	24	10	14		
1785	435	231	212	443	8	24	16	6		
1786	597	333	276	609	12	35	19	9		
1787	564	290	283	573	9	36	18	9		
1788	578	296	287	583	5	25	10	10		
1789	599	296	308	604	5	42	12	1		
1790	622	317	313	630	8	34	5	7		
1791	621	325	303	628	7	39	2	1		
1792	610	312	306	618	8	29	4	1		
1793	590	300	297	597	7	24	12	1	1 in 288	1 in 77.
1794	583	286	305	591	8	26	6	2		
1795	612	310	310	620	8	32	13	2		
1796	627	326	305	631	4	24	4	1		
1797	619	332	293	625	6	25	9	3		
1798	566	285	292	577	11	31	12	2		
1799	521	282	248	530	9	21	7	1	1 in 958	1 in 113.
1800	417	211	210	421	4	18	1	0		
Total ·	26202	13642	12871	26513	311	1073	795	391		

Proportion of Boys to Girls born in the Hospital is about 19 to 18.
Children Still-born in ditto, about   -   -   1 to 25.
Women having had Twins, about   -   -   1 to 84.

G

7. SOME miscellaneous observations on the yearly bills of mortality.

THE following statement was deduced in a coarse manner, from an average of about ten years, for the purpose of comparing generally the mortality occasioned by certain diseases, at the beginning, middle, and end of the eighteenth century; care being taken in each period to select such years, in which the whole number of deaths was nearly the same, viz. about 21,000.

	Beginning.	Middle.	End.
Abortive and Still-born -	600	570	750
Colic, Flux, Gripes, &c. -	1,100	135	20
Consumption - - - -	3,000	4,000	5,000
Dropsy - - - - - -	850	900	900
Evil - - - - - - -	70	15	8
Fever - - - - - -	3,000	3,000	2,000
Gout - - - - - -	26	40	66
Lunatic - - - - - -	27	75	70
Palsy, Apoplexy, &c. - -	157	280	300
Rickets - - - - - -	380	11	1
Small Pox - - - - -	1,600	2,000	2,000

To these might be added the article of convulsions. But it will appear upon enquiry, that the change has in this instance taken place in the name only, and not in the real

5

number

number of deaths. There can be little doubt, but the fame difeafes of children, which ufed formerly to be called chry-foms and infants, are now accumulated under the general head of convulfions. For we may obferve the decreafe of the two former articles to have taken place in a proportion very exactly correfponding with the increafe of the latter.

THE apparent increafe of the abortives and ftill-born will likewife in great meafure vanifh, if we refer them, as we ought, not to the burials, but to the births; the number of chriftenings, at the three periods above mentioned, bearing very nearly the fame proportion to each other, that obtains in thefe articles. Neverthelefs it muft be obferved, that the re-gifter of the Brownlow-ftreet Hofpital alfo exhibits a very fenfible increafe in the number of children ftill-born.

IT is not eafy to give a fatisfactory reafon for all the changes which may be obferved to take place in the hiftory of difeafes. Nor is it any difgrace to phyficians, if their caufes are often fo gradual in their operation, or fo fubtle, as to elude inveftigation. Of this kind are the origin and de-cline of the rickets. It is pleafing however to look back upon the progrefs of this difeafe, and trace it from year to year, as it has been growing continually lefs and lefs fatal.

THE fame obfervations are applicable to the evil alfo, unlefs we fuppofe its apparent decreafe ought rather to be attributed to a greater backwardnefs in acknowledging a complaint now univerfally believed to be hereditary.

OF

OF fevers I fhall have occafion to fpeak more particularly afterwards *.

THE view which prefents itfelf of confumptions, gout, lunacy, and palfy, muft be confeffed to be by no means favourable. The firft of thefe probably includes many other chronical diftempers, befides the pulmonary confumption. All of them feem to be almoft, if not altogether, unknown among barbarous nations, and may perhaps be the natural confequences of arts and civilization. As thefe again fhoot up into luxury and intemperance, their effects may well be expected to become proportionally more confpicuous. Dr. Rufh of Philadelphia has reported concerning the uncultivated nations of North America, that fevers, inflammations, and dyfenteries make up the fum of their complaints; and in particular, " that after much enquiry he had not been " able to find a fingle inftance of madnefs, melancholy, " or fatuity, among them (g)." In a fubfequent part of his work, the fame author, fpeaking of the pulmonary confumption, declares it to be " unknown among the Indians " of North America (h)." Likewife Mr. Park, in his Account of the Interior Parts of Africa, fays, that notwithftanding longevity is uncommon among the Negroes, their difeafes appeared to be but few in number : fevers and fluxes are the moft common, and the moft fatal.

THE

(g) Medical Enquiries and Obfervations, by B. Rufh, Vol. I. p. 25.
(h) Vol. I. p. 159.

The difcerning Sydenham had long before obferved, that " acute difeafes come from God, but chronical difeafes ori- " ginate with ourfelves *(i).*" Indeed we cannot doubt, that idlenefs and intemperance, with their long train of vices ; that covetoufnefs and anxiety, the neceffary attendants upon com- merce ; and manufactories, which fupply the materials for it ; muft all in their feveral ways be injurious to health. And it is not improbable, that they may very largely have contri- buted to fwell out the number of deaths under each of the difeafes in queftion.

It does not appear by the bills of mortality, that the num- ber of deaths from dropfy was increafed by the act paffed in 1690, for the encouragement of the diftillation of malt fpi- rits. Between the years 1718 and 1751, the average number is one-tenth greater than at any period before or fince. In 1751 the diftillation of fpirits was reftrained by act of par- liament, and the ufe of them checked by additional duties. Petitions were the year after fent up to parliament from va- rious parts of the kingdom, fetting forth the good effects of thefe regulations upon the morals and health of the people, and praying for a continuance of them. And the bills of mortality feem to confirm this, by the article of dropfy falling from above one thoufand annually to nine hundred, and ftill more by the reduction of exceffive-drinking from forty to five.

Of

(i) Morbi acuti Deum habent autorem, chronici ipfos nos.

Of the Weekly Table of Mortality.

It is not my defign to enter into a detail of all the parti
culars deducible from this table. The following general
refults however are fubmitted to the public, as a fpecimen of
the ufes to which it may be applied.

1. The whole number of deaths is greateft in January,
February, and March; and leaft in June, July, and Auguft.

I believe this is contrary to the received opinion, which
may perhaps have been handed down from thofe ages, when
the authority of Hippocrates, and Galen, fuperfeded the evidence of the cleareft facts (k).

Our table correfponds with the following one from Dr.
Short's obfervations, containing the aggregate of the monthly
mortality in London for fifteen years, from 1728 to 1743;
which I infert rather than the eleventh table of the fame
work, becaufe it affords the additional information of the
ages at which the feveral deaths took place, fhewing the different fluctuation at different periods of life.

(k) Celfus, who probably copied it from Hippocrates, fays, " Igitur faluber-
" rimum ver eft; proxime deinde ab hoc, hiems; periculofior æftas; autumnus
" longe periculofiffimus." Lib. II. Cap. 1.

	Under 2 Years.	From 2 to 5.	From 5 to 10.	From 10 to 20.	From 20 to 30.	From 30 to 40.	From 40 to 50.	From 50 to 60.	From 60 to 70.	From 70 to 80.	From 80 to 90.	90 and upwards.	TOTALS.
Jan. -	12,593	2,678	1,306	1,232	3,021	3,576	3,730	3,480	2,625	1,988	1,203	250	37,682
Feb. -	12,550	2,918	1,275	1,139	2,852	3,125	3,409	3,086	2,708	1,997	1,072	226	36,157
March	12,681	3,254	1,267	1,039	2,905	3,423	3,450	3,823	2,281	1,855	1,002	146	37,126
Apr. -	12,731	3,184	1,168	1,021	2,728	3,247	3,088	2,549	2,107	1,496	775	148	34,242
May -	12,268	3,194	1,269	1,004	2,494	3,991	3,046	2,628	2,174	1,427	775	148	34,410
June -	11,363	3,073	1,239	1,048	2,353	2,597	2,803	2,164	1,726	1,129	595	147	33,410
July -	10,063	2,889	1,195	952	2,261	2,748	2,622	2,259	1,558	1,021	528	107	30,197
Aug. -	12,684	2,897	1,170	926	2,241	2,426	2,755	2,543	1,555	1,049	481	114	28,210
Sept. -	13,563	3,101	1,168	1,081	2,401	2,933	2,850	2,558	1,787	1,212	617	102	30,829
Oct. -	13,832	3,069	1,190	1,080	2,344	3,215	3,125	2,372	2,030	1,439	786	104	33,375
Nov. -	12,010	2,867	1,169	1,097	2,685	3,378	3,255	2,924	2,313	1,511	850	108	34,590
Dec. -	12,319	3,055	1,297	1,136	2,617	3,416	3,609	3,090	2,504	1,876	846	122	34,181
												187	35,952
Total -	148,657	36,179	14,713	12,755	30,902	37,075	37,742	33,476	25,168	18,000	9,523	1,761	405,951

IF

IF we make allowance for the ſhortneſs of the month of February, that will appear in fact to be the moſt fatal of the twelve *(l)*.

IT may be ſuſpected perhaps at firſt ſight, that much of this ought to be attributed to the greater number of people reſident in London during the winter, than in the ſummer months. But what then ſhall we ſay to the following account collected by Dr. Short from the regiſters of five and twenty different country towns in England, including the burials of a great many years? For the reſult there alſo is very nearly the ſame, making allowance for thoſe irregularities, to which ſmall communities muſt of neceſſity be liable :

January - - - 16,932	July - - - 13,034
February - - 16,126	Auguſt - - - 12,795
March - - - 17,641	September - - 12,999
April - - - 17,670	October - - 13,629
May - - - 16,618	November - - 14,074
June - - - 13,680	December - - 15,658

THE monthly mortality at York agrees ſtill more perfectly with what has been obſerved of London. The annexed Table,

(l) The bills being ſent in every week makes the monthly mortality neceſſarily liable to ſome uncertainty. For, the ſame month which one year contains five weeks, may in the next contain only four. Theſe inaccuracies, which might be conſiderable in a compariſon of only two or three years, will diminiſh in proportion to the number of years which are eſtimated together.

Table, publifhed by Dr. White, fhews the number of burials in that city during feven years :

Jan. - 320	Apr. - 277	July - 220	Oct. - 237
Feb. - 282	May - 265	Aug. - 237	Nov. - 230
Mar. - 316	June - 274	Sept. - 225	Dec. - 292

The truth of thefe obfervations is moreover confirmed by the regifters kept at Edinburgh, and in Paris, and throughout the kingdom of Sweden (m).

On the other hand, at Marfeilles, and at Montpellier, the monthly mortality is ftated to vary as follows (n) :

	Marfeilles.	Montpellier.
January - - -	1,801 - - -	853
February - - -	1,597 - - -	774
March - - -	1,704 - - -	696
April - - -	1,681 - - -	694
May - - - -	1,504 - - -	673
June - - - -	1,465 - - -	769
July - - - -	1,881 - - -	1,038
Auguft - - -	1,849 - - -	1,114
September - -	1,725 - - -	1,100
October - - -	1,668 - - -	1,093
November - - -	1,765 - - -	1,040
December - -	1,659 - - -	950

Is

(m) Price on Reverfionary Payments, Vol. II. p. 271. 5th edit. where obferve that the words *former* and *latter* are tranfpofed.
(n) Mem. de la Soc. Roy. de Medicine, ann. 1777 & 1781.

H

Is the difference between this table and the former, occafioned by the different temperature of the places, from whence the accounts are drawn? In very cold climates, it is obvious that the coldeft part of the year is the feafon moft to be apprehended. For increafe the cold but a little, and it becomes quite inconfiftent with human life. But all the accounts we have of places fuffering from exceffive heat, agree in defcribing the autumn as the time of their greateft mortality. Now, it is reafonable to fuppofe with regard to temperature, as in moft other things, that fome degree of heat intermediate between thefe extremes muft be moft congenial to the human frame ; and that as any climate approaches nearer to the one, or the other limit, it will naturally partake more of their refpective inconveniences. This muft not be fo underftood, as if it were meant to preclude the operation of other caufes. Many circumftances peculiar to particular fituations, will no doubt often have a much fuperior influence in determining their falubrity, or unwholefomenefs. Still, where thefe are equal, there is fome ground to believe that the effects before mentioned do in fact take place.

2. UNDER two years of age, there die moft either in January February and March, or elfe in September and October.

It fhould be noticed that baptifms, and I prefume births, are ufually more numerous in the beginning of the year, than in the fubfequent parts of it ; as appears from the concurrent teftimony of the London Bills *(n*)*, and of thofe
kept

(n*) Short's Obf. p. 176.

kept in various parts of the country *(o)*, and from the regiſters of the whole kingdom of Sweden *(p)*.

THIS, if we reflect on the great mortality among children in the firſt two or three months from their birth, will in ſome meaſure account for the exceſs of their burials in the early part of the year. But when the number again increaſes in September and October, I apprehend that may truly be looked upon as the ſeaſon more eſpecially prejudicial to young children. It is at this time that bowel complaints are moſt prevalent in perſons of all ages *(p*)* ; and when it is conſidered how large a part they conſtitute of the diſeaſes of infants, it ſeems by no means improbable that the general cauſe ſhould be capable of producing this particular effect.

3. OF thoſe aged above ſixty years, by much the greateſt number die in the coldeſt months, and the feveſt in the middle of ſummer.

THERE can be little doubt but this ought to be attributed to the degree of cold. For univerſally old people, above all others, are moſt ſenſibly affected by it.

How much they differ from children in this reſpect, cannot be ſhewn more evidently than by a compariſon of their re-

ſpective

(o) Short's Obſ. p. 142.   *(p)* Price on Rever. Payments, Vol. II. p. 271.
(p*) See p. 54.

fpective numbers during the correfponding months of January 1795 and 1796. For of thefe two fucceffive winters, the month of January has in one inftance been the coldeft, and in the other the warmeft, of which any regular account has ever been kept in this country. The following Table exhibits at one view the mean height of Fahrenheit's thermometer in London for each week of the two years, together with the whole number of deaths, the deaths of perfons above fixty years old, and the deaths of children under two years :

1795.					1796.				
Week ending	Mean Heat.	Whole No of Deaths.	Aged above 60.	Under 2 Years.	Week ending	Mean Heat.	Whole No of Deaths.	Aged above 60.	Under 2 Years.
	Morn. Noon.					Morn. Noon.			
6 Jan.	25°—29°	244	51	66	5 Jan.	40°—46°	300	35	100
13 Jan.	26°—32°	532	139	129	12 Jan.	41°—49°	273	37	87
20 Jan.	24°—30°	637	145	141	19 Jan.	48°—53°	313	29	113
27 Jan.	19°—27°	543	143	128	26 Jan.	47°—52°	257	20	96
3 Feb.	25°—37°	867	239	153	2 Feb.	41°—49°	328	32	110
Total	23°—29°.4	2,823	717	617	Total	43°.5—50°.1	1,471	153	506

From hence it appears, Firft, that old perfons are affected by the cold much fooner than children; for in the very firft week of 1795, the proportion they bear to the whole number of of deaths is very nearly twice as great as in the succeeding year. Secondly, that while the mortality of the aged was five times greater in one year than in the other, the number of infants dying in the first year exceeded those in the second by only one-fifth part. So that the ratio of their respective increase was as five-and-twenty to one *(q)*.

It may be thought satisfactory to add, that the different mortality in the two years from which this comparison is drawn, cannot be accounted for from any accidental fluctuation of the number of people resident in London, nor from any irregularity in the bills themselves. On either of these suppositions, the christenings must have undergone a corresponding rise and fall; but they, during the same five weeks, neither exceeded their usual number in the one case, nor fell short of it in the other. In 1795, they amounted in this time to 1,622; and in 1796, to 1,650.

4. The number of deaths by palsies and apoplexies is in this country always greatest in winter.

This is probably because it is a disease of old age, and is consequently increased, and diminished, by the same causes, which influence the general mortality at that time of life. At Marseilles, not only the whole number of deaths, but those

also

(q) Some further account of the effects of cold may be seen in the Philosophical Transactions for the year 1796, p. 279.

alfo occafioned by apoplexies and palfies, are greateft in the fummer (r).

5. Consumptive people are of courfe fufferers by cold; and though they are not fo foon affected from this caufe as the afthmatic and aged, yet their numbers in the bills are always greateft in the cold months.

6. However the number of bowel complaints have been leffened within the laft hundred years, we ftill find them moft frequent in September and October.

In all hot countries thefe diforders are obferved to be more common, and more violent, than they are with us; and here in England they are moft prevalent after the hotteft fummers. This was the cafe in 1762, and again in 1789, 1790, and 1800. The time of year alfo when they principally occur in all climates, concurs to indicate fome connexion fubfifting between them and the ftate of the atmofphere. But what this is; whether the heat act thus upon the human body by occafioning inflammation, or relaxation, whether by profufe, or by morbid fecretions, or by what other means, I confefs myfelf unable to explain; notwithftanding the many pleafant theories about the nature of the bile, with which the books on Weft Indian difeafes in particular are filled.

7. The remaining difeafes, of which an account has been taken in the Table, feem to have no certain increafe or decreafe.

(r) Mem. de la Soc. Roy. de Med. 1777.

creafe. The meafles and fmall pox are exceedingly various, and without any apparent relation to the temperature, moifture, or other fenfible qualities of the feafons. The fame is in general true of fevers, with this exception, that in long and fevere winters they are certainly more numerous, for reafons which have been explained elfewhere *(s)*. Many poor families at fuch times being reduced to the neceffity of fhutting themfelves up, perhaps feveral together, in a fmall room, where they can afford to burn little or no fire, and where their beft defence againft the rigor of the feafon is to preclude as much as poffible all accefs to the external air.

CONVULSIONS are fo much made up of children's deaths, that they follow the fame courfe which has been obferved to take place under that article *(t)*.

FROM the weekly table of mortality we are enabled to correct fome popular errors, which are very generally prevalent. One of thefe is, that there is fomething peculiarly wholefome in a fharp froft *(u)*; another, that wet weather is noxious to the human body, and in particular that it is productive

(s) Medical Tranfactions, Vol. III. Obfervations on the Jail Fever, by John Hunter, M. D.

(t) " Prefque tous les enfants qui meurent avant l'age d'un an, et même de " deux, meurent avec des convulfions; l'on dit qu'ils font morts des convulfions, " et l'on a en partie raifon," &c. Tiffot, Avis au Peuple.

(u) Agreeable to this is the proverb, that " A green winter makes a fat " churchyard." See Ray's Proverbs.

ductive of putrid difeafes (x). After what has been ftated above, and what may be feen more at large in the Philo-fophical Tranfactions for the year 1796, there need not many arguments to difprove the firft of thefe opinions. The year 1797 affords a very favourable opportunity of afcertaining that the other is equally unfounded. That year, from the middle of May, was one of the wetteft ever remembered; yet fo far was this from rendering it prejudicial, much lefs peftilential, that whether we attend to the united fum of the deaths, or to the particular articles of which it is compofed, we fhall find reafon to believe it was in every refpect a healthy year. The fame was obferved alfo during the American war among the foldiers encamped at Coxheath in Kent, and it has occafionally been noticed at other times (y). The miftake has in both cafes probably originated from the known influence of heat and moifture in promoting putrefaction, and they are

not

(x) το μεν ολον οι αυχμοι των επομζριων εισιν υγιεινοτεροι. Hippocr. Aph. fect. 3. 15. Νοσηματα δε εν τησιν επομζρησιν ως τα πολλα γινεται πυρετοι τε μακροι, και κοιλιης ρυσιες, και σωτιδωες, &c. Ib. 16. Thus Hoffman in his Medicina Rationalis, " Aëri in-" falubritas, et ad ingignendos putridos morbos aptituto, inducitur ex crebra ac " diuturna aquarum inundatione." 4to. Vol. IV. p. 262. Many other autho-rities might be produced to the fame purpofe.

(y) Dr. Cuming of Dorchefter, in a letter addreffed to Dr. Fothergill upon the fubject of the influenza in 1775, has thefe words : " The autumn here was " very wet, as the quantity of rain that fell here during the months of Auguft, " September, October, and November, was exactly fourteen inches and twenty-" feven hundredth parts. This circumftance, joined to the mild temperature of " the air, made me expect difeafes of a putrid clafs, but in this I was happily dif-" appointed." Med. Obf. and Enq. Vol. VI.

not the only inftances of people being mifled by a name. But the cook and the chemift fhould be informed, that arguments drawn from a kitchen or a laboratory muft not be too confidently transferred to the operations of a living body.

THERE is reafon to think that another idea has been adopted by many people upon not much better grounds than the former. For it has been imagined, that neither heat, nor cold, are in themfelves pernicious, but that it is the rapid tranfitions from one to the other which are alone to be dreaded *(z)*. If this opinion carry with it an appearance of probability, fuch facts at leaft as are afforded by the bills of mortality at the end of the year 1796 and beginning of 1797 do in no wife correfpond with it. The great and fudden changes of temperature at that period are too recent to be forgotten. Before the middle of December 1796 it froze hard for feveral days, and prefently after thawed again : Chriftmas morning will long be memorable for the greateft cold perhaps ever experienced in England, Fahrenheit's thermometer in London ftanding below zero ; but in lefs than a week the fame thermometer was above 50°. The month of January following contniued to exhibit frequent and very uncommon variations of heat and cold ; yet the mortality all this time did not exceed its ufual limits.

THE fame opinion has been very commonly applied to the breaking up of a long froft ; people in general being more apprehenfive of bad confequences from the fucceeding thaw,

(z) ἀι μεταβολαι των ὡρεων μαλιϛα τικτϫσι νοϛηματα. Hippocr. Aph. 3, 1.

1

thaw, than from the cold itself. But this admits of a similar answer to the former. For the frost in the beginning of the year 1795 ended with the month of February, though the weather continued indeed to be colder than usual throughout the March following. We need only turn our eyes to the weekly table, to see how accurately this corresponds with the decrease of the mortality.

THE annexed extract from the bills of mortality for the year 1740, shews that the same effects took place likewise during the hard frost which is known to have set in the 24th of December 1739 (old style) and to have continued till the 16th of February 1740. In this case also, as in the former, the succeeding spring was cold and backward.

Week ending	Whole No of Deaths.	Aged above 60.
1 Jan.	543	95
8 Jan.	714	120
15 Jan.	777	163
22 Jan.	691	138
29 Jan.	728	136
5 Feb.	813	174
12 Feb.	780	170
19 Feb.	794	160
26 Feb.	771	146
4 Mar.	767	118
11 Mar.	591	104
18 Mar.	754	120
25 Mar.	620	95

BEFORE

BEFORE we take leave of this fubject, it fhould be noticed, that the numbers given in by the parifh clerks in the month of December, are lefs to be depended upon, than in any other part of the year. For, the yearly account being made up to the middle of that month, it frequently happens that parifhes, which have neglected to make any returns for many weeks together, give in at that time the fum of the baptifms and burials fince their laft report *(a)*. And as if the difcharge of this debt entitled them to contract new ones, fimilar omif-fions are more common in the two or three weeks imme-diately following, than at any other period.

SOME judgment may be formed of thefe inaccuracies, by comparifon with the weekly chriftenings. For whenever the burials fuffer any fudden increafe, or diminution, if the baptifms at the fame time undergo a correfponding change, threre will be reafon to attribute both rather to the irregu-larity of the parifh clerks reports, than to any real alteration in the health of the people.

(a) On the 13th of Dec. 1796, the parifh of St. George in Middlefex gave in the numbers for the whole year, amounting to 532.

PART II.

OF THE PLAGUE.

A TABLE,

Shewing how many died Weekly, as well of all Difeafes, as of the PLAGUE, in the Years 1593, 1603, 1625, 1636, and 1665.

From the Bills of Mortality.

	1593.		1603.		1625.		1636.			1665.	
	Total.	Plague.	Total.	Plague.	Total.	Plague.	Total.	Plague.		Total.	Plague.
June 2.	410	62	114	30	395	69	339	77	May 30.	399	17
June 9.	441	81	131	43	434	91	345	87	June 6.	405	43
June 16.	339	99	144	59	510	161	381	103	June 13.	558	112
June 23.	401	108	182	72	640	239	304	79	June 20.	611	168
June 30.	850	118	267	158	942	390	352	104	June 27.	684	267
July 7.	1440	927	445	263	1222	593	215	81	July 4.	1006	470
July 14.	1510	893	612	424	1781	1004	372	104	July 11.	1268	727
July 21.	1491	258	1186	917	2850	1819	365	120	July 18.	1761	1089
July 28.	1507	852	1728	1396	3583	2471	423	151	July 25.	2785	1843
Aug. 4.	1503	983	2256	1922	4517	3659	491	206	Aug. 1.	3014	2010
Aug. 11.	1550	797	2077	1745	4855	4115	538	283	Aug. 8.	4030	2817
Aug. 18.	1532	651	3054	2713	5205	4463	638	321	Aug. 15.	5319	3880
Aug. 25.	1508	449	2853	2539	4841	4218	787	429	Aug. 22.	5568	4237
Sept. 1.	1490	507	3385	3035	3897	3344	1011	638	Aug. 29.	7496	6102
Sept. 8.	1210	563	3078	2724	3157	2550	1069	650	Sept. 5.	8452	6988
Sept. 15.	621	451	3129	2818	2148	1672	1306	865	Sept. 12.	7690	6544
Sept. 22.	629	349	2456	2195	1994	1551	1229	775	Sept. 19.	8297	7165
Sept. 29.	450	330	1961	1732	1236	852	1403	928	Sept. 26.	6460	5533
Oct. 6.	408	327	1831	1641	833	538	1405	921	Oct. 3.	5720	4929
Oct. 13.	422	323	1312	1149	815	511	1302	792	Oct. 10.	5068	4327
Oct. 20.	330	308	766	642	651	331	1002	555	Oct. 17.	3219	2665
Oct. 27.	320	302	625	508	375	134	900	458	Oct. 24.	1806	1421
Nov. 3.	310	301	737	594	357	89	1300	838	Oct. 31.	1388	1031
Nov. 10.	309	209	545	442	319	92	1104	715	Nov. 7.	1787	1414
Nov. 17.	301	107	384	251	274	48	950	573	Nov. 14.	1359	1050
Nov. 24.	321	93	198	105	231	27	857	476	Nov. 21.	905	652
Dec. 1.	349	94	223	102	190	15	614	321	Nov. 28.	544	333
Dec. 8.	331	86	163	55	181	15	459	167	Dec. 5.	428	210
Dec. 15.	329	71	200	96	168	6	385	85	Dec. 12.	442	243
Dec. 22.	386	39	168	74	157	1			Dec. 19.	525	281
Whole Year	25886	11503	37294	30561	51578	35403	23359	10400	Whole Year	97306	68596

THE foregoing Table exhibits a melancholy, yet a very imperfect picture of what the people of this country formerly suffered from the Plague *(a)*. It is a subject which must ever be interesting to humanity, to trace out, as far as we are able, by what means it has 'happened, that a disease which was once so very destructive, should totally have disappeared for now considerably more than an hundred years. For this purpose, it will be necessary to enter at some length into the history of the circumstances attending its progress, and to look back if possible to its true origin.

MANY difficulties occur in the prosecution of this enquiry. Each country is unwilling to acknowledge herself the parent of such an odious offspring. From this part of Europe we are taught to look to Turkey for the source of this evil. Enquire there, and you are referred either to some vague report from the parts about the Caspian sea, or more commonly to Egypt. The Egyptians, on the other hand, will tell you they receive it sometimes from Turkey, but usually from Lybia, or Ethiopia ; in short, from places where there is nobody to contradict such a malicious report. In this manner Villani, who was at some pains to investigate the origin of

a great

(a) In the City Remembrancer is collected, from very respectable authorities, the best history of that dreadful time. An elegant account of similar miseries produced from the same cause in the city of Florence in the year 1348, may be seen in the Introduction to the Decamerone of Boccaccio.

a great plague in the fourteenth century, was referred at laſt
to China, and was told that it was there occaſioned by the
burſting of a great ball of fire attended with an uncommon
ſtench.

LEAVING theſe idle ſtories, if we direct our attention to
the places where in fact it has prevailed, we ſhall find its head
quarters always to have been the naſtieſt parts of dirty, crowded, ill conſtructed, large cities. Thus Grand Cairo, and Con-
ſtantinople, are never long free from it; and thus likewiſe
when it has attacked other places, where it is leſs common,
its firſt appearance has been among the loweſt of the people.
There, as on touchwood, the ſpark is eaſily kindled, and pre-
ſently blown into a flame. " Grand Cairo is crowded by a
" vaſt number of inhabitants, who for the moſt part live very
" poorly and naſtily. The ſtreets are very narrow and cloſe,
" and twenty or thirty live in one ſmall houſe. It is ſituated
" in a ſandy plain at the foot of a mountain, which by keep-
" ing off the winds, which would refreſh the air, makes the
" heats very ſtifling. Through the midſt of it paſſes a great
" canal, which is filled with water at the overflowing of the
" Nile, and after the river is decreaſed, is gradually dried up.
" Into this, people throw all manner of filth, carrion, &c.
" ſo that the ſtench which riſes from this and the mud toge-
" ther is inſufferably offenſive. In this poſture of things, the
" plague every year conſtantly preys upon the inhabitants,
" and is only ſtopped when the Nile by overflowing waſhes
" away this load of filth; the cold winds, which ſet in at

9   " the

" the fame time, lending their affiftance by purifying the
" air *(a*)*." The plague is very generally obferved to break
out at Conftantinople in that part of the city which is low
and marfhy *(b)*. And there, as every where elfe, " nitidæ
" ædes haud æque facile inficiuntur, ac fordidæ *(c)*." Black-
more takes notice that the impurity and filth, which accom-
panied the gallies and flaves at Marfeilles, filled the air with
offenfive fmells eafily perceivable by thofe that paffed along
the adjoining fhore : and in 1720, the plague broke out there
in a part of the town thronged by the pooreft people *(d)*. At
Aleppo, it always begins in the Keifarias and Judeda : the
former are fmall huts with few or no windows, which ftand
crowded together, and are inhabited by the loweft Arabs;
the latter are the dwellings of the inferior Jews, " whofe
" houfes are fmall; or if large, the different apartments are
" crowded with different families; many of them are more
" than a ftory below the level of the ftreet, in a condition
" half ruinous, dirty in the extreme, damp, and badly aired;
" and the wretched inhabitants are clothed with rags *(e)*."
In Holftein, in 1764, it firft appeared at Renfburg among the
prifoners, " propter delicta ad operas publicas damnatos *(f)*.
At Mofcow, it broke out " in domo ampliffima, quæ infer-
" viebat,

(a*) The City Remembrancer. This account is confirmed by Alpinus,
Pococke, Irwin, and a variety of other teftimonies.

(b) The City Remembrancer.

(c) Timone on the Plague at Conftantinople, Phil. Tranf. abr. Vol. VII.

(d) City Remembrancer.   *(e)* Ruffel on the Plague.

(f) Waldfchmidt de fingularibus quibufdam Peftis Holfatiæ. Haller Dif-
putat. Vol. V.

K

" viebat conficiendis pannis pro militibus ; tria hominum
" millia utriufq; fexus huic labori operabantur, quorum tertia
" pars circiter pauperrima in inferiore parte domus habita-
" bat *(g)*. In London, the plagues of 1626, and 1636,
broke out at Whitechapel, a part of the town which abounded
with poor, and with flaughter-houfes : that of 1665 is faid to
have broke out firft at St. Giles's ; and there it would probably again break out, if ever we fhould fuffer fuch another
calamity.

THERE can be no doubt that the plague is infectious ; and
it would be eafy to point out the way in which it may be introduced by foreign contagion. Indeed the correfpondence of
the dates of our laft great plagues, with thofe of Amfterdam,
affords a ftrong prefumption, either that one of thefe cities
muft have received the infection from the other, or that both
of them received it from fome common fource. Yet it fhould
be remembered, that it is by no means fo eafily imported, as
the fears of moft people incline them to believe. Nor, becaufe a perfon labouring under the plague may communicate
the poifon to goods, and fuch goods afterwards to other people,
does it by any means follow that either of thefe effects muft
neceffarily take place. We have many reafons to perfuade us
to the contrary. For if a fingle bale of cotton be fuppofed
capable of introducing the difeafe ; who could efcape from
the infection, which had been harboured in the furniture of a
whole city during the continuance of a plague ? Neverthelefs

we

(g) Mertens, Obfervationes Medicæ de Pefte Mofcuenfe.

we read that when the plague was in Italy, the Neapolitans
ufed no artifice to purify either their goods, or houfes ; yet
the difeafe ceafed among them as entirely as in the beft regulated towns. So Profper Alpinus, fpeaking of the plague in
Egypt, fays, " Junio vero menfe, qualifcunque et quanta-
" cunque fit ibi peftilentia, fole primam cancri partem ingre-
" diente, omnino tollitur, quod multis plane divinum effe non
" immerito videtur. Sed quod etiam valde mirabile creditur,
" omnia fupellectilia peftifero contagio infecta tunc nullum
" contagii effectum in eam gentem edunt." In Syria alfo,
where it's returns are very frequent, yet from September to
March it is fcarcely ever feen : and Dr. Ruffel tells us that in
the winter time, when infected perfons have come to places
about Aleppo, fome of whom have died in the families where
they lodged, the diftemper by fuch means was not propagated. Diemerbroeck likewife obferves, that when the plague
has been excited out of its proper feafon, it has not fpread.
The fame thing is confirmed by the foregoing Table, and I
believe by the hiftories of the plague in all large towns of
Europe. For its chief force has always been felt in the fummer and autumn *. Afterwards, " le carnage diminue, la
" maladie

* May not this influence of the feafons on difeafes, be the real caufe of the
ftrange and contradictory accounts we have received concerning the cure of the
Yellow Fever in the Weft Indies ? Accounts which only agree in this, that the
moft obvious methods of treatment are wrong. It is reafonable to fuppofe, that
phyficians there would firft make trial of the remedies moft approved in fimilar
difeafes in other places ; yet we find they all failed. And why ? Becaufe the epidemic was then at it's height. But afterwards, all their different modes of practice as
univerfally fucceeded. For when the difeafe began to decline, the mortality of it-

felt

" maladie devient plus traitable, les accidens font moins
" preffans, & le plus grand nombre de ceux qui en font
" atteints, echappe au danger *(g*)*."

But a proper ftate of the air is not the only circumftance
neceffary to promote the operation of contagion. During the
epidemical conftitution, it is highly probable, that good diet,
and good fpirits, and cleanlinefs, and frefh air, and proper
clothing, and exercife, may all contribute to render the body
lefs fufceptible of difeafe. The feeds of which, like thofe of
vegetables, will then only fpring up and thrive, when they
fall upon a foil convenient for their growth. " In folam
" plebem, ut femper fere accidit, fæviit peftis Mofcuenfis ;
" inter nobiles, et ditiores mercatores, neminem fere, præter
" paucos valde incautos invafit *(h)*." Likewife at Marfeilles, " la pefte fit fes plus grands ravages dans les quartiers
" habités par le menu peuple *(i)*." The fame has been
found to be true univerfally.

Every medical man will readily acknowledge the difficulty of afcertaining the true caufe of almoft any difeafe ;
and with refpect to that under confideration, the difficulty is

on

---

felf became much lefs ; and of thofe who died, moft lingered on for a confiderable
time beyond their ufual period. Which exactly correfponds with what has at all
times been reported of the plague, under every variation of medicine, and
climate.

(g*) Fournier, Obf. fur la Pefte.
(h) Mertens, de Pefte Mofcuenfe.
(i) Traité de la Pefte.

on many accounts much increased. For interest, the most powerful of all motives in a commercial state, interferes in opposing our enquiries. The early risings of the plague are always endeavoured to be concealed, in order to prevent that interruption of trade, which necessarily takes place, where it is publicly avowed. " La peste n'est reconnue dans une ville, " que lorsque ses ravages se multiplient. D'abord elle n'en- " leve que peu de malades ; leur petit nombre n'attire pas l'at- " tention ; les doutes occupent quelque tems l'esprit : le mal " est-il averé, des raisons d'interêt le font deguiser. C'est ainsi " que la maladie fait des progrés secrets, elle se glisse," &c. *(k)*.

Now, that the plague was ever actually bred in London, it might be odious to assert, and would be impossible to prove. But to any one who reflects upon it's frequent returns in this capital until the latter end of the seventeenth century, and it's total absence since, notwithstanding the great increase of our trade by which it was supposed to be imported ; it must I think appear probable, that if it's origin were derived from foreign contagion, at least it's propagation ought in great measure to be attributed to some predisposition of the town in those days, which has since been corrected. Any improve- ments which our quarantine laws may have undergone, are by no means adequate to such an effect *(l)*. But there have not been wanting many more powerful causes.

IN

(k) Traité de la Peste.

(l) See this matter discussed in Mr. Howard's Observations on Lazarettos, and in Eton's Survey of the Turkish Empire.

IN 1389, the ſtreets of London were ſo abuſed with common lay-ſtalls, to the great annoyance of the citizens, that
a proclamation was made throughout the city by authority of
parliament, " that no perſon whatever ſhould preſume to lay
" any dung, guts, garbage, offals, or any other ordure, in any
" ſtreet, ditch, river, &c. upon penalty of twenty pounds, to
" be recovered by an information in chancery." In 1569,
when the plague was in London, orders were iſſued " to
" warne all inhabitants againſt their houſes, to keep channels
" clear from fylth (by onlie turning yt aſyde) that the water
" may have paſſage." And Eraſmus, in a letter to Franciſcus,
Cardinal Wolſey's phyſician, aſcribes the ſweating ſickneſs,
which was a ſpecies of plague (m), and the plague, from
which England was hardly ever free, in great meaſure to the
incommodious form, and bad expoſition of their houſes, to the
filthineſs of the ſtreets, and to the ſluttiſhneſs within doors.
" Conclavia ſola fere ſtrata ſunt argilla, tum ſcirpis paluſtri-
" bus (n), qui ſubinde ſic renovantur, ut fundamentum maneat
" aliquoties annos viginti ſub ſe fovens ſputa, vomitus, mic-
" tum

(m) The years in which the ſweating ſickneſs more particularly prevailed,
were 1485, 1506, 1517, 1528, 1551. Dr. Caius muſt probably have been miſ-
taken when he mentions in his treatiſe, " De Ephemera Britannica," one circumſtance entirely contrary to what has occurred in any plague of which I have
yet ſeen an account, " Nam miſeram illam et jejunam plebeculam belli paciſque
" laboribus_duratam, aut omnino non attigit, aut ſine gravi noxa vel peri-
" culo."

(n) Hentzner, ſpeaking of the preſence chamber at Greenwich palace in the
time of Queen Elizabeth, obſerves that " the floor, after the Engliſh faſhion,
6   " was

" tum canum et hominum, projectam cerevifiam, et pifcium
" reliquias, aliafque fordes non nominandas." This picture
of the naftinefs of the town will be yet heightened by confidering the ftate of the buildings before the great fire of 1666.
The ftreets were narrow, and crooked, and many of them un-
paved; the houfes were built of wood, and lofty; they were
dark, irregular, and ill contrived; with each ftory hanging
over the one below, fo as almoft to meet at top, and thereby
preclude as much as poffible all accefs to a purer air; they
were befides furnifhed with enormous figns, which by hanging into the middle of the ftreet, contributed not a little to
prevent all ventilation below. The fewers at the fame time
were in a very neglected ftate, and the drains all ran above
ground. Add to which, the metropolis, which now enjoys
fuch a plentiful fupply of water laid into every houfe, had
till many years fubfequent to the bringing in of the New
River in 1613, been but fcantily furnifhed with this firft
of luxuries (o).

WE are enabled to form fome judgment of the effect of
this ftate of things upon the health of the inhabitants, by confidering

" was ftrewed with hay." The fame cuftom is alluded to by Shakfpeare, and
Ben Johnfon; alfo by Dryden, in his Tale of the Cock and the Fox:
" Her parlour window ftuck with herbs around,
" Of fav'ry fmell; and *rufhes ftrew'd the ground.*"
It is probable that in earlier times this had not been peculiar to England. Boccaccio, defcribing the villa to which the perfonages of his Decamerone retired
from the plague at Florence, in the middle of the fourteenth century, fays, " Il
" quale tutto fpazzato, e nelle camere i letti fatti, ed ogni cofa de fiori, quali
" nella ftagione fi potevano avere, piena, e *di giunchi giunchata,*" &c.

(o) This account of London is chiefly taken from Maitland's Hiftory.

fidering the nature of the difeafes which were then prevalent.
Burnet fays, in his Hiftory of the Reformation, that in the
laft year of Queen Mary's reign, " Intermitting fevers were
" fo univerfal and contagious, that they raged liked a plague."
Have we any idea of fuch a thing at prefent? Morton affures
us, that remittent fevers were very deftructive for feveral
years before the great plague of 1665. In 1658 Oliver Crom-
well died of this fever: and he tells us his own father alfo
died of it, and that himfelf and his whole family were infected, " matrem pientiffimam, fratres, forores, fervos, ancillas,
" nutrices conductitias, quotquot erant intra eofdem nobif-
" cum parietes, ac fere omnes ejufdum, ac vicinorum pago-
" rum incolas, hoc veneno infectos, et decumbentes vidi."
He proceeds to fay, that the cold weather afterwards checked
this difeafe ; yet the feeds of it feem to have been by no means
deftroyed: they ftill continued to fhew themfelves under a
different form ; " durante enim bruma, intermittentes, quar-
" tanas, tertianas, quotidianas, ab ejufdem veneni mitiore
" gradu oriundas, fere æque epidemias videre erat, ac in au-
" tumno συνεχεας, feu remittentes ; neque mehercule fæviente
" gelu penitus defecerunt iftæ febres continentes. Atque
" equidem hancce febrem hoc pacto fub typo συνεχεΘ., præ-
" fertim fimplicis et legitimæ, quotidianæ fcilicet, vel ter-
" tianæ, maxime vulgarem fuiffe, et tempore autumnali plus
" minus epidemiam, ufque ad annum 1664 obfervavi." He
informs us likewife, that in the two years immediately fucceeding the great plague, dyfenteries were very frequent ;
fo that in the autumn of 1667 " civitas fere univerfa hoc
" morbo

" morbo correpta videbatur, atque fingulis feptimanis 345
" plus minus fluxu et torminibus confecti fatis cedebant."
Afterwards we are told the fame difeafe returned every autumn attended by nearly the fame mortality. Major Graunt,
whofe Obfervations on the Bills of Mortality were publifhed
in 1662, fays, " The difeafes which, befides the plague,
" make years unhealthful in this city, are, fpotted fevers,
" fmall pox, dyfentery; called by fome the plague in the
" guts; and the unhealthful feafon is autumn." From Sydenham we learn that from 1661 to 1664 agues were epidemical in London, and again from 1677 to 1685. This may
be looked upon as the flighteft of the effects of putrid
moifture: and even to this we are at prefent almoft ftrangers,
unlefs among thofe who come from the marfhy parts of the
country. The fame author informs us the dyfentery was
epidemical four years together; and the bills of mortality of
that time fhew the fum of the deaths under the titles of bloody
flux and griping in the guts, which muft both of them be
confidered as dyfentery, never to have been lefs than 1,000
in a year, and fome years to have exceeded 4,000; and for
five-and-twenty years fucceffively, from 1667 to 1692, the
number every year amounts to above 2,000. At the fame
time we are told that in the jail of Newgate a contagious
fever ufed to break out annually in hot weather; and that the
fame was true of moft jails in Europe *(p)*. Befides the well-
known black affize at Oxford in 1577, there happened a
fecond black affize only two years after, from which upwards

(p) The City Remembrancer.

L

wards of 500 perfons died. And Dr. Plott fuggefts as a probable reafon for the unhealthinefs of Oxford at that time,
that the city was very much thronged, and all manner of
cattle uſed to be killed within the walls, and their dung and
offals were ſuffered to lie in the public ſtreets. The true
ſcurvy, which is now unknown in London, is alſo juſtly
attributed, along with other cauſes, to a putrid atmoſphere.
And it is of this that Hodges ſpeaks in his account of the
plague of 1665, when he tells us, " epidemica multo ante
" apud nos affectio ſcorbutica." So Hentzner, in his Travels
at the time of Queen Elizabeth, obſerves that the Engliſh
" are often moleſted with the ſcurvy." Willis, who wrote a
particular treatiſe on this ſubject, deſcribes it in all its charac-
teriſtic features as being very common : " ægritudo multis in
" locis (Angliæ) endemia, et ubique fere ſporadica." Charle-
ton alſo declares, " ſcorbutus in his regionibus ſeptentrionali-
" bus eſt morbus endemius." Many other authorities might
be produced to the ſame effect.

EXAMINE then how far the plague kept pace with theſe
other diſeaſes. In the early part of our hiſtory, a great number of years are ſpecified as plague years (q). In the fourteenth, fifteenth, and ſixteenth centuries, there ſcarcely paſſed
ten years without a conſiderable plague. The greateſt plague
years of the ſeventeenth century were 1603, 1625, 1636,
and 1665 ; in which the mortality is reported to have
been

(q) See the City Remembrancer.

been refpectively 36,000, 35,000, 10,000, and 68,000 *(q*)*. But we muft not imagine the difeafe was accidentally imported juft at thofe periods, and that at other times London was perfectly free. The fame bills of mortality, and the teftimony of all hiftory, pofitively contradict fuch an opinion. In 1603, the deaths by the plague amounted, as we have faid, to 36,000; in 1604 there died by the fame difeafe 900; in 1605, 400; in 1606, 2,000; in 1607, 2,000; in 1608, 2,000; in 1609, 4,000; in 1610, 1,800; and from 1640 to 1648, the number was every year above 1,000. I would not be underftood to infinuate that the mortality was always fo great, as in the years here mentioned. There might pafs fome years without any perfon dying of the difeafe. I am difpofed to believe however, that the number of thefe muft have been much fewer than moft people are aware of. Maitland, in his Hiftory of London, declares that for five-and-twenty years before the fire of 1666, the city had never been clear from the plague. And from the year 1603, when the regifter begins, till 1670, the bills of mortality exhibit only three years entirely free : though it muft be confeffed the mortality in fome others is fo fmall as to leave room to doubt whether the caufe of thofe deaths may not have been mifreprefented.

THE

(q*) There is reafon to believe that thefe numbers, great as they appear, are confiderably under the truth. Lord Clarendon fays, that " many, who could " compute very well, concluded there were in truth double that number who " died." Hift. of his own Life.

THE plague therefore, as well as other putrid difeafes, prevailed in a very high degree in times when we know the condition of the town to have been moft offenfively dirty. And it is pleafing to obferve how the health of the inhabitants returned, in proportion as this caufe of their complaints was removed. In September 1666, while the plague was yet unfubdued, happened the memorable fire of London. It raged for feveral days together, till it had confumed every thing from the Tower to Temple Bar. This, which was at firft looked upon as a fcourge from Heaven, has fince proved indeed a moft gracious blefling. Great pains were taken, and much encouragement was given by the king, to obtain proper plans for rebuilding the city. The ftreets were widened; the fign-pofts ordered to be " fixed againft the balconies, or fome " other convenient part of the houfe," inftead of hanging acrofs; directions were prefcribed for levelling the ftreets " for the more eafy and convenient current and conveyance " of the waters;" proper places were appointed for common lay-ftalls; ceft-pools were ordered to be " made and conti- " nued to every grate of the common fewer, to receive the " fand or gravel coming to the fame, fo to prevent the " choaking thereof;" orders were iffued refpecting the " fel- " lowfhip of carmen, who fhould fweep and cleanfe the " ftreets, lanes, and common paffages, from dung, foil, filth, " and dirt;" all perfons were forbid to lay in the ftreets " any dogs, cats, inwards of beafts, cleaves of beafts' feet, " bones, horns, dregs or drofs of ale or beer, or any noifome " thing, upon pain of ten fhillings for every offence:" it was

ordered

ordered alfo, " that no man fhall feed any kine, goats, hogs, or
" poultry in the open ftreets ;" " that no man fhall caft into
" ditches or fewers, grates or gullets, of the city, any manner
" of carrion, ftinking flefh, rotten oranges or onions, rubbifh,
" dung, &c. &c." that no man " fhall make or continue
" any widraughts, feat or feats for houfes of eafement over,
" or drains, into any common fewers, &c." and other regulations were enforced to the fame effect *(r)* ; by which means
many of the former inconveniences and nuifances were reme-
died. So that in a few years the new town rofe up like a
phœnix from the fire with increafed vigour and beauty. Nor
did the benefit end there ; for it produced in the country a
fpirit of improvement which had till then been unknown, but
which has never fince ceafed to exert itfelf.

LET us now again turn our eyes towards the ftate of
difeafes. Morton relates of the autumnal fever : " Febris
" συνεχης genuina ab anno 1665 (in quo peftis, veneno ad gra-
" dum fumme deleterium provecto, caput fuum extulit) fere
" per biennium profligata difparuit, nec amplius recedente
" fole graffata eft ut ante." And again : " Venenum febri-
" ferum anno 1673 quadantenus mitefcere et cicurari vide-
" batur, et mitius huc ufque (1692) eft." And the gradual
decreafe of the dyfentery, which we have fhewn to have
been fo very deftructive, though already taken notice of in
the former part of this effay, is too much to the purpofe
not to be repeated. For taking together the three difeafes of
bloody

(r) See Maitland's Hiftory of London.

bloody flux, colic, and gripes, their decline from the beginning of the eighteenth century has been nearly as follows :

From 1700 to 1710 the average is about 1,070 annually.

1710 to 1720	770
1720 to 1730	700
1730 to 1740	350
1740 to 1750	150
1750 to 1760	110
1760 to 1770	80
1770 to 1780	70
1780 to 1790	40
1790 to 1800	20

THE fame bills of mortality, fo far as they may be trufted
in an article confeffedly liable to great inaccuracy, fhew the
decline of fcurvy likewife to have been very rapid. The firft
twenty bills, that is, from the year 1657 to the year 1677,
give an average of fixty deaths every year under this head;
whereas fince the beginning of the eighteenth century, the
number has fcarcely exceeded five, or fix. It's decreafe
among our failors has been much more remarkable. For I
have been informed by one of the phyficians to the Haflar
hofpital near Portfmouth, that their wards, which ufed to be
crowded with fcorbutic patients, now do not receive above
twenty in the whole year. And in this inftance nobody can
hefitate to attribute the change to the attention that has of
late years been paid to the cleanlinefs, ventilation, and diet of
our navy. It is probably from a fimilar attention, that the

9   number

number of fevers reported in the bills of mortality, have in the courfe of the laft fifty years been reduced from 3,000 to 2,000 annually.

But to return to the plague. In 1666, there are reported to have died in London by this difeafe 1,998 ; in the year follow-ing, 35 ; and the year after that, 14 ; fince which time the number has never exceeded five ; and the laft year it is men-tioned at all in the bills is 1679 ; notwithftanding the popu-lation, and the trade of London, have been fo rapidly increaf-ing from that time to this *(t)*.

It may be worth while to obferve, that the plague was formerly by no means confined to the metropolis. In 1625, it alfo broke out at Oxford ; and moreover feized the feamen and foldiers on board the fleet, and obliged them to relinquifh the objeĉt they were at that time engaged in,

(t) The number of people in London feems never to have fuffered any material diminution in confequence of the great mortalities which from time to time took place. It appears by the bills of mortality, that in two years after-wards both the chriftenings and burials, and we may fuppofe therefore the inha-bitants of London, regained their ufual ftandard. For, " if there be encourage-" ment for an hundred in London, that is, a way how an hundred may live " better than in the country, and if there be void houfing there to receive " them, the evacuating of a fourth, or a third part of that number, muft foon be " fupplied out of the country ; fo as the great plague doth not leffen the inha-" bitants of the city, but of the country, who in a fhort time remove themfelves " hither, fo long, until the city, for want of receipt and encouragement, regur-" gitates and fends them back." Major Graunt's Obfervations.

in, of intercepting the Spanish galeons. In 1665, every town within twenty miles of London was more or less infected, and moft of the principal towns in England, befides fome parts of Ireland. In 1391, it was moft feverely felt in Norfolk, and at York; in 1643, it broke out at the fiege of Reading; in 1645, it was at Leeds; and in 1646, at Newark, Stafford, and Totnefs. About the fame time it likewife occafioned a great mortality in Ireland. From an expreffion ufed by Lord Clarendon, in his Hiftory of the Rebellion, one may form fome judgment how familiar this difeafe muft formerly have been in Briftol. He is fpeaking of the reafons which induced the Prince of Wales to appoint certain commiffioners to meet him at Bridgewater rather than at Briftol in April 1645, and obferves that " Briftol was " thought at too great a diftance from the Weft, befides that " the plague began to break out there very much for the " time of year, &c." Yet we find this did not deter the prince from returning thither the very next week.

At the time the plague was fo deftructive in England, it feems to have raged with equal violence in other parts of Europe; and probably from the fame caufe. The hiftories of thofe ages are full of the phyfical and political miferies which prevailed. And in proportion as the nations of Europe have become civilized; and agriculture, with the arts of peace, has been cultivated, this diforder has gradually difappeared.

In

In the fifteenth century, at Bourdeaux, " il regné prefque " tous les ans une maladie peftilentielle, qui força plufieurs " fois le parlement, pour fe fouftraire à la contagion, de tenir " fes féances dans d'autres lieux de fon reffort *(u)*." The following *(u*)* are all of them mentioned as having been plague years at Drefden; viz. 1504 -5, 1511 -12, 1521, 1535 -36, 1547, 1563 -64, 1571 -72, 1585 -86, 1591 -92, 1607, 1627 -28, 1632 -33 -34 -35 -36 -37. In 1502 the difeafe was at Bruffels; 1511 at Verona; 1525 in Germany; 1531 and 1534 in France; 1539 in Switzerland; 1542 at Breflaw; 1550 at Bafil; between 1550 and 1553 it fpread itfelf fucceffively over almoft all the habitable world; 1559 it was in Holland; 1563 it was in Germany, and again in 1566; 1564 in Savoy; 1566 and 1568 at Milan; 1568 at Paris; 1572 at Bafil; 1575 at Milan; 1576 at Venice; 1580 at Marfeilles; 1593 it was in Holland and the Low Countries; 1596 and 1597 in Germany; 1603 it was again in Holland, alfo in 1609, and in the latter year in Denmark; 1618 at Bergen; 1619 in Denmark; 1622 at Amfterdam, where it continued for eight years; 1623 it was at Montpellier; 1625 at Leyden, in Denmark, and in Germany; 1628 it was at Lyons; 1629 and 1630 at Montpellier; 1631 at Dijon; in 1630 it was befides in Denmark, and at Chriftiana in Norway, and at Parma, Verona, and other parts of Italy;

(u) Hift. de la Soc. Roy. de Med. Vol. I. 188.

(u*) It may be proper to obferve, that the dates of the plague which are here collected, are none of them inferted without fome authority; though it feemed unneceffary to multiply the notes by fo many diftinct references.

M

Italy; from 1635 to 1637 it was in the Netherlands, and the latter year at Prague; in 1649 more than 200,000 persons are said to have perished by this disease in the southern provinces of Spain; 1649 and 1650 it prevailed at Marseilles; 1650 it was also in Ireland; 1652 at Cracow; 1653 in Poland, and Prussia; 1654 at Copenhagen; 1655 at Amsterdam; and in the course of the same year, and the three following, it was in many places in the south of Europe; 1660 it was in Scotland; 1663 and 1664 at Amsterdam, and Hamburgh; 1668 in Flanders; 1670 in Italy; 1679 at Vienna; 1680 at Leipsic; 1684 in Norway; 1685 at Leghorn. In 1622 the mortality by the plague at Amsterdam (at that time equal to about one-third of London) was 4,000; in 1623, 6,000; in 1624, 12,000; in 1625, 6,800; in 1626, 4,400; in 1627, 4,000; in 1628, 4,500. Felix Platerus, physician at Basil, in Switzerland, about 1580, gives an account of seven different pestilential fevers which afflicted that city in the space of seventy years. Thomas Bartholin mentions five that raged in Denmark in his time (1660). And Forestus relates that in his time (1570) the plague was frequent at Cologn and Paris; and refers the cause to the multitude of the inhabitants, and the nastiness of the streets. In the life of Erasmus we read " ob pestilentiam multis annis " (Parisiis) perpetuam, singulos annos redeundum erat in " patriam—tandem ubi totum annum sæviret pestis, coactus " est Lovanium commigrare." By another account Paris is said to have been infected eight times between the years 1480 and 1590: in 1607 two hospitals of reserve, St. Louis

I   and

and St. Anne, were erected on purpose to receive patients in times of the plague, or other great calamities. They were opened on account of the plague in 1619, 1631, 1638, 1662, and 1668, since which that disease has been unknown there. We are informed that about the same time Paris was paved, and the streets were widened, and the city began to be kept cleaner (w). To the same purpose it is said, in the Histoire de la Societé Royale de Medecine (année 1786, p. 215) " Il " suffit de se rappeler, à ce sujet, ce grand nombre d'epide- " mies desastreuses et pestilentielles dont parlent nos histo- " riens des derniers siecles, et qui, n'etant dues qu'à la mal- " propreté des habitations mal äerées et des rues mal pavées, " ont disparu quand le gouvernement a consideré que ces " objets ne devoient pas échapper à ses regards, et meritoient " une part à sa solicitude." In another place we read that the city of Thouloufe " morbis malignis sæpe vexabatur : sed " tandem (A. D. 1757) dilatatis urbis plateis et compitis, " purgatis quotannis stercoribus, liberoque aëri transitu con- " cesso, a contagio libera evasit urbs (x)." Of the condition of these two cities formerly, we may form some judgment by the following quotation from Diemerbroeck : " Fætidissi- " mam platearum, cloacarum, et sterquilinionum illuviem, " ad multorum morborum, et imprimis malignarum febrium " inductionem, ac pestiferi contagii propagationem, pluri- " mum facere, docet experientia : sicut de Parisiorum urbe
" testatur

(w) Rapport des Commissaires chargés par l'Académie de l'examen du projet d'un nouvel Hôtel-Dieu. 1786.

(x) Linnæi Amænitates, Vol. IV.

" teftatur Palmarius, et Quercetanus de urbe Tholofana."
Likewife of Marfeilles, at the time of the laft plague, we are
told, " la ville de Marfeille eft fort peuplée, & fort refferree ;
" les maifons y font fort petites, &c. &c. *(y)*.

INDEED moft towns of any antiquity retain fome traces of
the fame kind. " The moft ancient part of Madrid is neareft
" to the river Manzanares, with narrow and contracted
" ftreets, crooked lanes, and blind allies, like thofe ftill
" vifible in London, but more efpecially in Paris, where no
" extenfive conflagration hath confumed the rude monuments
" of art erected by the remote progenitors who inhabited the
" infant city *(y*)*." Some cities of Europe, which from natural or political caufes have been backward in adopting the
improvements of modern times, yet continue to exhibit a
more lively picture of former manners. " Till within the
" laft two years Cracow was not wholly paved ; and no-
" thing can be fo execrable as the prefent paving, which
" fcarcely deferves the name. There is not a fingle lamp
" in the place. No precautions are ufed to cleanfe the ftreets ;
" which of courfe become infectious in fummer, and almoft
" impaffable in winter *(aa)*."

IT cannot be fuppofed that this difeafe has worn itfelf out,
as feems to have been the cafe with fome others. For it
continues

(y) Traité de la Pefte. *(y*)* Townfend's Spain.

(aa) Wraxall's Memoirs of the Courts of Berlin, Drefden, Warfaw, and
Vienna, in the years 1777, 1778, and 1779.

continues ftill in Turkey at leaft as frequent as at any former period; and even in the eighteenth century has been feverely felt in Poland, Hungary, and Pruffia, between 1702 and 1709; in Germany, Livonia, and Sweden, 1710; in Holland, 1711; at Vienna, 1712, 1713, 1714; at Hamburgh alfo, 1714; in the South of France, 1720; in Sicily, 1743; in Hungary, 1756; in Denmark, 1764; in Ruffia, 1771; and perhaps at Cadiz, 1800 *.

It is obfervable, that at it's firft breaking out, the difeafe has never been known to be the plague. It has, moreover, very generally been preceded by a fevere putrid fever. This at leaft we know to have been the cafe at Nimeguen *(z)* in 1635, in London *(a)* 1665, at Marfeilles *(b)* 1720, in Holftein *(c)* 1764, at Mofcow *(d)* 1771. " Les medicins de " Livourne confultés fur la nature de la maladie qui defolait " l'equipage

---

* I know not how far fome epidemical fevers of America deferve to be ranked under this head. Such have been defcribed in Philadelphia 1699, 1741, 1747, 1762; in Virginia 1737, 1741, and 1778; four different times at Charleftown in South Carolina, viz. 1732, 1739, 1745, 1748; in New York 1791; in Philadelphia 1793; in Baltimore 1794; at Norfolk in Virginia 1795; in New York 1795, 1796, and 1798; and the latter year likewife very feverely in Philadelphia; and again in Baltimore 1800. The mortality, in proportion to the number of inhabitants, appears in fome inftances to have equalled what the fevereft plagues have occafioned in Europe; and there is reafon to believe the fame want of attention to cleanlinefs, and pure air, may have been a principal caufe of both difeafes. See *A fhort Account of the Plague in Philadelphia,* by *M. Carey,* 1794. Alfo *Weld's Travels in America.*

(z) Diemerbroeck.   (a) Sydenham.

(b) Traité de la Pefte.   (c) Waldfchmidt.   (d) Mertens.

" l'equipage du vaiſſeau auquel on attribua la naiſſance de la
" peſte de Marſeille, le regarderent unanimement comme une
" ſimple fievre maligne *(e)*. Of this preceding fever at Mar-
ſeilles it is ſaid, " on obſerva dans le cours de ces fievres, des
" bubons, des charbons, des parotides : des morts ſubites
" avoient deja annoncé quelque changement ſingulier dans les
" corps, ou dans les ſaiſons." Waldſchmidt, who had before
obſerved, " ſolent plerumque peſtis contagium præcedere
" morbi alii, febres mali moris, et peſtilentiales," tells us,
theſe diſeaſes then deſerve the name of plague, " quando
" plures communi aura et mutuo commercio fruentes ſimul
" ægrotant, & plerique moriuntur : quod ſi accedant ſumma
" virium proſtratio, bubones, carbunculi, vibices, petechiæ,
" tunc demum certi eſſe poſſumus de luis præſentia." Diemerbroeck, among the ſigns which frequently precede the
plague, enumerates " morbi epidemii mali moris, dyſenteriæ
" valde malignæ et contagioſæ, et imprimis febres putridæ
" maligniſſimæ, et purpuratæ, plurimiſque lethales." He
moreover mentions particularly the gradual progreſs of theſe
fevers into the true plague; " prædiĉta febris peſtilens, in-
" dies majora incrementa ſumens, magis magiſque in pejus
" mutabatur, donec tandem in apertiſſimam peſtem tranſiret."
In like manner Morton, ſpeaking of the poiſon that produced the remittent fever, which he deſcribes to have been
prevalent in London for ſome years previous to 1665, ſays,
" Venenum ſeſe recolligens, et mirum in modum auĉtum,
" hanc συνεχη in peſtem funeſtiſſimam et diriſſimam inopi-
" nato

(*e*) Preface to Mem. de la Soc. Roy. de Medicine.

" nato mutavit." And as the plague originally blazes forth
from the embers of malignant difeafes ; fo at it's termination
it feems again to fubfide into them. " Febres quæ anno poft
" graviorem peftem uno aut altero paffim graffantur, pefti-
" lentes effe folent ; et licet aliquibus veræ peftis notis def-
" titutæ, tamen ejufdem naturam ac indolem quam pluri-
" mum referunt, nec non confimilem medendi rationem fibi
" vindicant *(f)*." Sir John Pringle has likewife related,
upon the authority of Dr. Mackenzie, who refided thirty
years at Conftantinople, that the annual peftilential fever of
that place, which very much refembles that of our jails and
crowded hofpitals, is only called the plague when attended
with buboes and carbuncles *(g)*. In Syria alfo in the winter,
and early in the fpring, the characteriftic eruptions are often
wanting *(h)*. At Mofcow, a putrid fever had been epidemic
for three years preceding the plague ; but as foon as the
plague broke out, the fever ceafed *(i)* : which is agreeable
to the obfervations made at all times upon this difeafe.

It is from confiderations like thefe, and from the fimilarity
of the circumftances under which both difeafes are found to
prevail, that the plague has been thought to be nothing more
than a high degree of putrid fever. Sydenham himfelf,
fpeaking of the " febris maligna " which ufhered in the
plague of 1665, fays, " Cum ipfiffima pefte fpecie convenit,
" nec ab ea nifi ob gradum remiffiorem difcriminatur." In
the

(f) Sydenham.   *(g)* Army Difeafes.
(h) Ruffel on the Plague.   *(i)* Mertens.

the fame manner Rothman, in his account of the plague at
Stockholm in 1710, obferves, " Febris ardentis (*i. e.* malignæ)
" naturam et proprietates rite qui noverit, huic et ipfa peftis,
" utpote gradu tantum ab hac differens, ignota non erit."
And it is worthy of notice, how, according to the bills of
mortality, the article of fever in general, but efpecially the
fpotted fever, always increafed and decreafed along with the
plague.   Of the latter thère never died more than four in a
week before the plague began ; but afterwards the number
frequently exceeded an hundred: nor was this by any
means peculiar to London.   Diemerbroeck relates the fame
of the plague in the Netherlands ; and Gockelius is quoted
by Dr. Browne as obferving, that fome foldiers, returning
from Hungary in 1665, fpread the infection of the plague
about Ulm and Augfburg, where he then lived, " and befides
" the plague, they brought along with them the Hungarian
" and other malignant fevers, which diffufed themfelves
" around the neighbourhood, whereof many died."   And
more particularly Beerwinckel, who was a phyfician at Ham-
burg during the plague in the year 1714, " Sæpiffime in cura
" peftis obfervavimus febres petechiales in peftem, atque
" hanc in illas tandem degeneraffe ; & fi bubones retroceffe-
" rint, febrem petechialem fere ordinarie ortam fuiffe.   Hinc
" colligo, materiam bubonum et harum petechiarum, fi non
" unam eandemque, parum tamen differentem fuiffe."
There is reafon therefore to fufpect either that this fever
muft have been the fame with the true plague, or that the
plague often paffed under the name of malignant fever.
                                                    M. Defgenettes,

M. Defgenettes, the principal phyfician who attended Bona-
parte's army in the late expedition to Egypt, fays of the
plague, " Qu'il n'a pu, malgré les renfeignements nombreux
" qu'il a cherchés, en obtenir une hiftoire fatisfaifante ; il
" s'eft auffi apperçu que l'on confond generalement dans le
" pays toutes les fievres peftilentielles, qui font tres variées,
" et forment un genre, avec la pefte proprement dite,
" qui eft une efpece bien circonfpecte (j)." The difference
between them feems to confift in this ; that the one is
more infectious, is generally attended with buboes and
carbuncles, is quicker in it's progrefs, and is more frequently fatal. But it muft be obferved, that this diftinction is
applicable only to the general courfe of each difeafe, not to
particular cafes ; for there ftand recorded inftances of other
fevers which have feemed even in thefe refpects to fall little
fhort of the true plague. Diemerbroeck confeffes there is no
pathognomonic fign of the plague ; for that buboes and
plague fores, which have by fome been confidered as fuch, are
fometimes met with in other difeafes, and are at other times
wanting in this. Accordingly his defcription of the " figna
" & fymptomata peftem comitantia," is agreeable to what
we are yet well acquanted with in the jail fever. Beerwinckel defcribes the appearance of the plague at Hamburgh
in 1714 in the fame manner; yet that this difeafe was the
true plague, is very evident from the defcription he afterwards gives of the buboes, and carbuncles, and other tokens.
Rothman, in his hiftory of the plague at Stockholm in 1710,

again

(j) Mem. fur l'Egypte.

N

again confirms the fame account, and concludes " dari autem
" revera peftem fine bubone, carbunculo, macula, &c. non
" eft quod quis dubitet." In Jofeph Browne's Treatife of the
plague are likewife enumerated " the fpecial figns of perfons
" infected with the plague according to Ludovicus Gardinius
" and Eberhardus Gockelius ;" which contain nothing more
than is common to all putrid fevers : there is even no mention made of buboes or carbuncles, till you come to the fucceeding chapter upon " the figns after death." Of the great
plague in London it was faid, " the practitioners in phyfic
" ftand amazed to meet with fo many various fymptoms
" which they find among their patients ; one week the ge-
" neral diftempers are blotches and boils ; the next week as
" clean fkinned as may be ; but death fpares neither : one
" week full of fpots and tokens, and perhaps the fucceeding
" bill none at all (k)."

In the directions publifhed by the College of Phyficians
refpecting the plague of 1665, the following defcription is
given of the different eruptions, which ufed to diftinguifh the
difeafe at that time :

" Directions for the Searchers.

" 1. They are to take notice whether there be any
" fwellings, rifings, or botch, under the ear, about the neck
" on either fide, or under the armpits of either fide, or the
" groins ;

(k) Extract of a Letter from John Tillifon, Sept. 14, 1665, to Dr. Sancroft;
preferved in the Britifh Mufeum, Vol. 3785. *Harl. Mss.*

" groins ; and of it's hardnefs, and whether broken, or un-
" broken.

" 2. WHETHER there be any blains, which may arife in
" any part of the body in the form of a blifter, much bigger
" than the fmall pox, of a ftraw colour, or livid colour,
" which latter is the worfer : either of them hath a reddifh
" circuit fomething fwollen round about it, which circuit
" remains after the blifter is broken, encompaffing the
" fore.

" 3. WHETHER there be any carbuncle, which is fome-
" thing like the blain, but more fiery and corrofive, eafily
" eating deep into the flefh, and fometimes having a black
" cruft upon it, but always encompaffed about with a fiery
" red, or livid, flat and hard tumour, about a finger breadth
" more or lefs : this and the blain may appear in any part of
" the body.

" 4. WHETHER there be any tokens, which are fpots
" arifing upon the fkin, chiefly about the breaft and back,
" but fometimes alfo in other parts : their colour is fome-
" thing various, fometimes more reddifh, fometimes inclining
" a little toward a faint blue ; and fometimes brownifh
" mixed with blue ; the red ones have often a purple circle
" about them, the brownifh a reddifh."

ON the other hand, Morton, who muft have been well
acquainted with both difeafes, fays of the common autumnal
fevers, " nonnunquam in primo infultu malignæ extiterunt,
" parotidibus, bubonibus, authracibus, cæterifque maligni-

" tatis

" tatis indiciis notatæ." He afterwards diftinguifhes thefe from the plague, by their not being fo readily propagated by contagion. Dr. Mead obferved of thofe who with difficulty efcaped from fome of the worft forts of the fmall pox, " hi " omnes, quod memorabile eft, fub finem morbi grave aliquid " paffi funt; nam aut furunculis frequentibus in corpore " obortis, aut tumoribus in glandulis fub auribus et axillis " qui ægre fuppurarent, excruciabantur;" and Dr. Freind, fpeaking of a bad fever which fpread on board the fleet in the year 1705, fays, " in perpaucis parotides, aut abfcef- " fus circa inquen orti morbum folverunt (kk)." Sir John Pringle likewife takes notice, that when the courfe of the jail fever is long, it fometimes terminates in fuppurations of the parotid. " I remember," fays he, " one inftance of a " fwelling of this kind on both fides, without any previous " indifpofition, when the perfon not fufpecting the caufe, and " applying difcutient cataplafms, was, upon the tumour's fub- " fiding, feized with the hofpital fever, which was then fre- " quent." Dr. Lind alfo obferves, " We have, though but " rarely, feen in very violent infections a fwelling of the pa- " rotid glands, which for the moft part was unattended with " a fever; notwithftanding that, fuch as were in this " manner feized, commonly died." He adds, " I had reafon " to fee at Winchefter many of the French prifoners, who " were infected with a fever of a very malignant kind, at- " tended with buboes in the groin and armpits, and other " peftilential fymptoms." Dr. Donald Monro likewife met

with

(kk) De Febr. Comm. 2.

with many examples of parotids towards the decline of the malignant fever, and in three patients faw critical fwellings of the groin *(l)*. But a more ftriking example than any of thefe is related by Sir John Pringle, which indeed fhews that the jail fever under circumftances favourable to it's progrefs, may vie with the plague itfelf in contagion and malignity. " The fick from the army hofpitals being ordered
" to remove from Germany to Flanders, they were em-
" barked in bilanders, to be carried to Ghent. During the
" voyage the fever having acquired new force by the con-
" finement of the air, by the mortifications, and other putrid
" effluvia, it became fo virulent, that above half the number
" died in the boats, and many of the remainder foon after
" their arrival. It's refemblance to the plague was further
" evinced by this memorable incident : a parcel of old tents
" being fent on board the fame bilanders with the men,
" were ufed by them for bedding : thefe tents, in order to
" be refitted, were put into the hands of a tradefman at
" Ghent, who having employed twenty-three Flemifh jour-
" neymen about the work, loft feventeen of them by the dif-
" temper, though they had no other communication with
" the infected."

In many refpects then there muft be allowed to fubfift a ftrong refemblance between thefe difeafes. The authors of the *Traité de la Pefte* declare, " Nous pouvons même avancer
" hardiment, qu'on y reconnaitra facilement le caractere des
" fievres,

(l) Monro's Military Hofpital.

" fievres malignes les plus ordinaires ; du moins leur rapi-
" dité & quelques accidens feront les feules chofes qui diftin-
" gueront ces fievres de la pefte." Their affinity may perhaps be compared to that which a common ague bears to the
remittent fever. And if an accumulation of the caufes of
putrid fevers cannot produce a plague ; at leaft it feems capable of producing a predifpofition to it, where the leaven of
the plague, however introduced, prefently exalts the reign-
ing fever into it's own nature ; fuperadding it's proper characteriftic fymptoms to fuch as are common to both difeafes.
Conformably to this notion, Diemerbroeck takes notice, " **Si**
" quifquam alio quodam morbo corriperetur, intra viginti
" quatuor horas peftis illi morbo adjungebatur, ita ut toto
" anno vix ullus morbus pefte incomitatus vifus fuerit." We
have affurances that fome complaints have in this manner
been engrafted as it were upon the ftock of previous difeafes.
" In autumn 1757, feveral foldiers were brought into the
" hofpital at Portfmouth with a diforder compounded of the
" autumnal and jail fever : for when thofe men, upon being
" feized with the common fever of the feafon, were con-
" fined to the holds of the crowded tranfports, their diftemper
" affumed that form *(m)*." So upon admitting into an hofpital one perfon with a flux, feveral other patients in the
fame ward have had this fymptom added to their other
complaints *(n)*. And Dr. Blane has obferved generally, that,
fuppofing a fhip's company be predifpofed to acute diftempers, and one man or more ill of a dyfentery be brought on
board,

(*m*) Pringle's Army Difeafes.   (*n*) Lind on Fever and Infection.

board, this will become the prevailing difeafe *(o)*. Sydenham's works abound with inftances of the fame kind : as,
where he is fpeaking of an epidemical cough, " Veruntamen
" qualifcunq ie fuerit febris ftationaria, quæ illum annum
" funeftat, atque per id temporis dominatur, nova hæc febris
" ftatim in ejus nomen ac familiam adoptatur, ejufdem
" ubique genio obfequens, licet fymptomata quædam adhuc
" retineat, a tuffi, quam habuit parentem, pendentia."

WE have fhewn then, that the ftreets of London were
formerly very clofe, and dirty, and the houfes within very
flovenly : we have fhewn alfo in a former part of this
effay *(p)*, that the inhabitants lived crowded together, probably not lefs than twice as many in the fame fpace they
occupy at prefent. By pointing out the difeafes which prevailed in thofe times, we have fhewn what influence this
ftate of things appears to have had upon the health of the
people ; and how the effect, and the caufe, have declined together : we have fhewn from the teftimony of eye-witneffes
how nearly the plague is allied to thefe other difeafes ; how
common it was at the fame time with them ; and how it
has alfo difappeared with them : we have fhewn moreover,
that the prefence of infectious matter is not alone fufficient to
make the difeafe epidemical ; but that fome concurrent ftate
of the air, and of the human body, is likewife neceffary. I
flatter myfelf therefore we fhall be juftified in drawing this
conclufion : that our long exemption from the plague, is not
fo

(o) Difeafes of Seamen.   *(p)* Page 66.

fo much to be attributed to any accidental abfence of its exciting caufes, as to our own change of manners, our love of cleanlinefs, and ventilation, which have produced amongft us, I do not fay an incapability, but a great unaptnefs, any longer to receive it.

F I N I S.

E S S A Y II.

ON THE

SMALL-POX and MEASLES*(a)*.

———————

TABLES *shewing the* NUMBER *of* DEATHS *occasioned by the* SMALL-POX, *in the several Periods of Life, and different Seasons of the Year, together with its* COMPARATIVE FATALITY *to* MALES *and* FEMALES; *extracted from the Register of the Collegiate or Parish Church in* MANCHESTER, *and from other* BILLS *of* MORTALITY.

ACCURATE and comprehensive bills of mortality furnish a variety of the most curious and important observations; and it is to be lamented that they are not universally adopted. The general uses to which they may be applied, have been fully pointed out; and a plan for the establishment of them has been proposed to the consideration and correction of the public *(b)*. It is one part of this plan, that the register of burials shall not only

———————

(a) Inserted in the London Medical Observations and Inquiries, vol. V. p. 270.   *(b)* See vol. I. p. 428.

contain

contain a lift of the difeafes of which all die, but alfo exprefs particularly the numbers dying of each difeafe, *in the feveral divifions of life, and different feafons of the year.* The following tables will illuftrate the advantages, which may be derived from this improvement.

An Account of DEATHS *by the* SMALL-POX, *during* SIX YEARS, *viz. from* 1768 *to* 1774; *collected from the Regifter of the Collegiate Church at* MANCHESTER.

TABLE I.

Ages.	Males.	Females.	Annual Deaths by the Small-Pox.		Deaths by all Difeafes.
From Birth to 3 Months.	2.	2.	A. D.		
From 3 Months to 6 Months	9.	8.	1769.	74.	549.
			1770.	41.	689.
- - - - - to 1 Year	51.	68.	1771.	182.	678.
2.	103.	113.	1772.	66.	608.
3.	55.	55.	1773.	139.	648.
4.	33.	26.	1774.	87.	635.
5.	18.	16.			
10.	17.	12.			
20.	1.	0.			
30.	0.	0.			
Total	289.	300.		589.*	3807.

I. THIS

* THIS account of the annual deaths by the fmall-pox from 1768 to 1774, differs from the printed bills of mor-

tality;

I. This table is formed from a very accurate regifter, and affords a ftriking view of the difparity in the ravages of the fmall-pox, at different periods of life. The proportion of deaths under the age of three months is extremely fmall; and I think we may conclude, that this diftemper rarely occurs in the early part of infancy. For children in that tender feafon are neither in the way of infection, nor does experience fhew that they are much difpofed to receive it. Dr. Monro informs us, that of twelve infants, inoculated within a fortnight, after their birth, not one had the variolous eruption *(c)*. In the fecond ftage of infancy, the fatality of the fmall-pox is fomewhat increafed; but the advancement proceeds afterwards with amazing rapidity. For, during the eighteen months which next fucceed, the number of deaths amounts to 335; which is more than one half of all that occur through the remainder of life. At this period, therefore, we may prefume that the body is peculiarly liable to the difeafe; and the violence and malignity of it are aggravated by the breed-

tality; which make the number amount to 586, and not to 589. But it has been extracted from the church regifter with a degree of care and attention not ufually beftowed upon the printed bills; and the accuracy of it may, I believe, be relied upon.

(c) Monro on Inoculation, p. 25.

ing

ing of teeth, and by the general irritability of the nervous fyftem. But the firft dentition is ufually completed before the end of the third year; at which time the fmall-pox appears, by the table, to become confiderably lefs mortal. And its declenfion is not lefs rapid than its pro-grefs, as the conftitution improves in vigour, and as thofe decreafe in number who are liable to its attack.

In the year 1773, the fmall-pox raged with great violence in the town of Warrington; and I have procured from my friend Mr. John Aikin, an exact account of the number and ages of thofe who died of it. This account coincides with the foregoing table, and confirms many of the conclufions which are deducible from it.

DEATHS BY THE SMALL-POX
AT WARRINGTON IN 1773.

TABLE II.

Ages.				Numbers.
Under	1	Month		0.
From	1	to	3 Months	4.
	3	--	6 - - -	6.
	6	-- 12	- - -	39.
From	1	to	2 Years	84.
	2	--	3 - - -	33.
	3	--	4 - - -	18.
	4	--	5 - - -	15.

F 4   From

Ages.				Numbers.
From 5	to	6	Years	4.
6	--	7	- - -	2.
7	--	8	- - -	2.
8	--	9	- - -	4.

None above.   Total 2 1 1.

II. THE fmall-pox, by table I, appears to have been more fatal to female than to male children, and the difference is confiderable under the age of two years. At Warrington, two thirds of all who died of this difeafe in 1773 were females. Thefe facts are fomewhat extraordinary; as it has been fully evinced by a variety of obfervations, that the life of males is much more frail than that of females *(d)*, and particularly in the period of infancy *(e)*. They alfo contradict the following remark of Baron Van Swieten: *Cum autem muliebre Corpus mollius et laxius fit corpore virili, hinc, cæteris paribus, & in his mitior effe folet hic morbus.*

Comment. vol. V. p. 16.

III. THE comparative mortality of the fmall-pox at Manchefter, Warrington, and Chowbent, in the different feafons of the year, may be eftimated by the following table.

(d) SEE Dr. Price's Treatife on Reverfionary Payments, *paffim*; alfo the preceding Obfervations on the State of Population in Manchefter, and other adjacent Places.

(e) Ibid.

TABLE

T A B L E   III.

Months.	MANCHESTER, From 1768 to 1774.	WARRINGTON, 1773.	CHOWBENT, From 1767 to 1773.	Total.
January, February, March,	160.	21.	17.	198.
April, May, June,	137.	135.	7.	279.
July, Auguſt, September,	147.	51.	2.	200.
October, November, December.	145.	4.	1.	150.

SYDENHAM has obſerved, that the ſmall-pox, when it is mild and regular, uſually commences about the vernal equinox, in thoſe years in which it is epidemic; but that it begins earlier when it is of an irregular and more dangerous kind. No one can doubt, that variations in the moiſture, dryneſs, temperature, and other qualities of the air, muſt influence a diſeaſe, which is always of an inflammatory, and often, in its laſt ſtages, of a putrid nature. But the progreſs of it cannot be regulated by the ſeaſons, becauſe it is derived from contagion; the communication of which frequently depends upon accident, is confined to no period of time, and is varied by its degrees

of

of malignity.   During the late vifitation of the
fmall-pox at Warrington, the ftate of the atmofphere went through all poffible changes, but
with no perceptible difference in the circumftances of the difeafe *(f)*.

IV. DURING the period of time included in
the firft table, the fmall-pox was twice epidemical in Manchefter; and the deaths by it
amount nearly to one fixth and a half of thofe
occafioned by all other difeafes.   But it may be
proper to remark, that the poor of this town are
chiefly buried at the collegiate church; and this
diftemper proves much more fatal to them than
to perfons of better rank, from their want of
cleanlinefs, and their prejudice in favour of a hot
regimen.   In London, from 1762 to 1772, the
average proportion of deaths by the fmall-pox is
109 in 1000, or about a ninth of the whole.
And at Ackworth, a country parifh near Ferry-
bridge in Yorkfhire, the proportion during
twenty years, viz. from 1747 to 1767, is as 1 to
19; two hundred and fixty-three perfons having
been buried, fourteen of whom died of the fmall-
pox.   Were fuch accounts to be collected from
different places, and at different periods of time,
it is probable, that farther variations in the fata-

(f) See Philofophical Tranfactions, vol. LXIV. p. 439.

lity

lity of this difease would be difcovered *(g)*.
But from its leaft deftructive ravages we may
derive arguments of fufficient force, in favour of
inoculation. And the two firft tables may perhaps furnifh fome ufeful information, concerning
the particular feafon of life in which this practice
will be moft expedient, and attended with the
greateft profpect of fuccefs.

(g) BARON Van Swieten has given the following remarkable account of the proportion of deaths by the fmall-pox, in
feveral fchools and hofpitals at Vienna. *Ratione fubducta,
patet, quod numerus omnium, qui in his locis variolis decubuerunt,
fit* 355, *et quod ex hoc numero feptem mortui fuerint. Adeoq;
proportio mortuorum ad numerum fanatorum eft ut* 1. *ad* 50.
*circiter. Si autem de hoc mortuorum numero detraherentur tres
aegri, quorum mors folis variolis adfcribi nequit, tunc certe proportio mortuorum ad fanatos foret ut* 1. *ad* 89. *circiter.*

Van Swieten. Comment. vol. V. p. 145.

MR. BEW, an ingenious apothecary in Manchefter, informs
me, that he attended feventy patients the laft year (1774)
under the natural fmall-pox, of which number only two died.
They were chiefly children above the age of two years; and
the cool regimen was ftrictly purfued in the treatment of
them.

In the fecondary fever of the fmall-pox, I have known a
warm bath, prepared of a decoction of chamomile leaves and
flowers, with a proper quantity of butter-milk added to it,
produce the happieft effects. It cleanfes the fkin from the
putrid *fordes* which covers it; foftens the puftules; opens
the pores; promotes perfpiration; and proves highly refrefhing to the patient.

IF

V. If we regard only the ftate of the body, the fitteft period for the ingraftment of the fmall-pox feems to be between the age of two and four in healthy children, and of three and fix in thofe who are tender and delicate. The powers of nature are then fufficiently vigorous; perfpiration is free and copious; the irritability of the body is diminifhed; the vifcera are found and unob-ftrufted; the mind, though aftive and lively, is not difturbed by violent emotions; the teguments are properly extenuated; and the fibres are nei-ther too tenfe nor too lax for the variolous erup-tion. To thefe important advantages may be added, that at this age the child is both a proper fubjeft for preparatory medicines, and for fuch as may be deemed neceffary during the courfe of the diftemper. But other confiderations, befides the ftate of the conftitution, demand our atten-tion. The rifque of receiving the natural fmall-pox by infeftion appears to be very great during the fecond year of life; and the fatality of the difeafe at this period is highly alarming. To avert fuch impending danger, the inoculation of healthy and vigorous children, at the *age of two or three months*, feems to be advifeable, efpecially in large towns. An earlier period might com-plicate the fmall-pox with the jaundice, thrufh, gripes, diarrhœa, and other diforders incident to the firft ftage of infancy; and a later feafon may

fuperadd

fuperadd the fever, convulfions, and other fymptoms of dentition. But I have enlarged upon
this fubject in the former volume, to which I
refer the reader *(b)*.

My friend Dr. Haygarth, to whom I communicated the preceding *Tables of the comparative mortality of the fmall-pox, &c.* has adopted
the plan, and purfued the fame inquiry at
Chefter. His ftatement will fhew how exactly
our obfervations agree.

CHESTER, 1774.

Total of deaths by the fmall-pox, - 202.
Deaths by the fmall-pox under 1 year old, 51.

(b) See vol. I. p. 230.

In a letter from the Hon. and Rev. Mr. Stuart, rector of
Luton in Bedfordfhire, to Sir William Fordyce, dated March
1, 1788, it is faid, that of 1215 patients inoculated in that
parifh, only five died, and thofe at the following ages.

Perfons.	Ages.		
1	9 weeks old,	thrufh.	
1	7	ditto.	
1	12	ditto.	
1	16	ditto.	of a fit.
1	5	ditto.	

viz.

viz.

		Males.	Females.
Under 1 month,		0.	0.
Between 1 and 2 months,		1.	1.
2 and 3,		1.	0.
3 and 6,		2.	2.
6 and 9,		12.	10.
9 and 12,		6.	16.
Total		22.	29.

TABLES *of the* COMPARATIVE MORTALITY *of the* MEASLES *from* 1768 *to* 1774, *collected from the Register of the Collegiate Church in* MANCHESTER.

T A B L E   I.

Ages.	Males.	Females.	Seasons.	Total of Deaths by all Diseases, during 6 Years.
From Birth to 3 Months	1.	1.	Jan. Feb. March } 17.	
From 3 Months to 6 Months	3.	0.		
1 Year	6.	4.	April May June } 51.	
2.	17.	14.		
3.	17.	8.	July Aug. Sep. } 16.	
4.	4.	3.		
5.	2.	7.		
10.	0.	2.	Oct. Nov. Dec. } 7.	
20.	0.	1.		
30.	0.	1.		
Total	50.	41.	91*.	3807.

THIS

* THIS, like the first table of the small-pox, differs in the total of deaths by the measles, from the printed bills of mortality.

THIS table requires no comments. The proportional mortality of the meafles, in the feveral periods of life, and various feafons of the year, is obvious at the firft view. It is equally evident alfo, that this difeafe differs from the fmallpox, in being much more fatal to males than to females.

DURING the fpring and fummer months of the year 1774, the meafles were epidemical in Manchefter, and proved fatal to a confiderable number of children. They were of the regular kind, fo well defcribed by Sydenham; but it was not unufual for violent peripneumonic fymptoms to occur, five, fix, or even eight days after the difappearance of the eruption. Under thefe circumftances venæfection, bliſters, and the Seneka root were found to be very efficacious remedies.

tality. I have therefore defired Mr. Holme, one of the clerks of the collegiate church, a very intelligent man and a good arithmetician, to revife the church regifter; and after the moft careful infpection, he aſſures me, that the numbers in both tables are perfectly accurate. He fays, " The printed " bills of mortality are exact as to the number of deaths, " and the divifion of males and females; but when the dif- " orders are counted over, and the general amount is taken, " there is often a miftake in the fum total. And, as it is " a great trouble and difficulty to difcover wherein the " error lies, and as few perfons pay any regard to this part " of the bills, it is common to add the number deficient to " fome of the diforders, fo as to make the whole agree."

I prefcribed

I prescribed the Peruvian bark with great success to many of my patients under the measles, combining it with demulcents, and the saline mixture; and premising venæsection when the signs of inflammation were urgent. The practice of giving the bark in this disease was first introduced by Dr. Cameron, a very eminent physician at Worcester. He observes that it prevents the recession of the morbid acrimony, and continues the efflorescence on the skin, sometimes so long as the twelfth day *(i)*. By this salutary operation, the cough and other inflammatory symptoms are in a great measure obviated; and the patient is freed from all danger of a peripneumony, the fatality of which Sydenham describes in such strong terms. It is many years since I first adopted the method of cure recommended by Dr. Cameron; and experience has afforded me the fullest conviction of its safety and efficacy, in all ordinary cases. During the late epidemic, not a single instance occurred to me of the peripneumony succeeding the measles, when the bark had been employed. But my assistance was desired in the last stage of fifteen unfortunate cases of this kind, in which the common antiphlogistic and pectoral course had been pursued.

(i) Medical Museum, vol. I. No. 37, p. 281.

THE

THE meafles, when violent in degree, or ill treated, frequently lay the foundation of hectic fevers, or pulmonary confumptions. For as the infection is moft probably conveyed by infpiration, the lungs become inflamed, a cough enfues, tubercles or a vomica are formed, and the patient finks under a lingering, painful, and incurable difeafe. To obviate thefe evils, inoculation was propofed about fifteen years ago, and practifed, in feveral inftances, with confiderable fuccefs by Dr. Home. The forenefs of the eyes was mitigated by it, the cough abated, and the fever rendered lefs fevere. His method of communicating the infection was by applying, to an incifion in each arm, cotton moiftened with the blood of a patient labouring under the meafles (k). But the morbillous matter has fince been ingrafted by means of lint, wet with the tears, which flow from the eyes in the firft ftage of this diforder. For thefe laudable endeavours to extend the benefits of inoculation, the public is highly indebted to Dr. Home; and it is to be lamented, that fo little attention has been paid to this valuable improvement of the healing art.

THE following table fhews the annual medium of deaths by the fmall-pox and meafles, from 1754 to 1774, compared with the deaths under

(k) Home's Medical Facts and Experiments.

two years of age by all difeafes, and with the general amount of births and deaths during the fame period of time. It is collected from the printed bills of mortality, publifhed yearly at Manchefter.

TABLE II.

Years.	Small-Pox.	Meafles.	Under 2 Years of Age.	Total of Deaths.	Births.
From 1754 to 1758	64.	21.	209.	651.	678.
to 1764*.	95.	10.6.	213.	639.	731.
to 1769.	98.	9.6.	229.	659.	827.
to 1774.	102.	21.6.	242.	651.	1002.
Total	359.	62.8.	893.	2600.	3238.

THIS table comprehends fo long a term of years, that the inferences which it affords would be no lefs indubitable than important, if we could entirely rely upon the accuracy of the *printed bills of mortality*. I apprehend, however, the errors of thefe bills are not confiderable;

---

* I AM not in poffeffion of the bill of mortality for the year 1760; which is therefore omitted in this table.

and

and that the following conclusions, with respect to Manchester, may be admitted as approaching very near to TRUTH.

I. ONE in *nine,* of all whose births are registered at baptism, dies of the SMALL-POX; and nearly *one* in *fifty-two* of the MEASLES. It should be observed, that the births considerably exceed the burials at Manchester.

II. THE deaths by the MEASLES are to the deaths by the SMALL-POX, as *one* to *five* and *eight tenths.*

III. THE number dying under two YEARS OF AGE, of all diseases, is to the number baptized, as *one* to *three* and *six tenths.*

IV. THE number dying under two YEARS OF AGE is to the total number of deaths, as *one* to *two* and *nine tenths.*

V. THE deaths by the SMALL-POX are to the deaths by all diseases, nearly as *one* to *seven* and *a quarter.*

VI. NEARLY *three fifths* of those who are carried off by the SMALL-POX die under the age of two years (see table I. of the small-pox); and *one* in *four* of all that die under two years of age fall victims to this disease.

VII. HALF of the deaths occasioned by the MEASLES happen under two years of age; and the proportion which this number bears to the general deaths, under the fame period, is nearly as *one* to *twenty-eight*.

MANY other very important corollaries may be deduced from this and the preceding tables; but I wifh rather to excite, than to anticipate the inquiries of the intelligent reader.

FEB. 1, 1775.